1987

NEIL A. PARENT

GENERAL EDITOR

REPRESENTATIVE FOR

ADULT EDUCATION

DEPARTMENT OF

EDUCATION

UNITED STATES

CATHOLIC

CONFERENCE

CHRISTIAN ADULTHOOD

A CATECHETICAL RESOURCE

In its 1986 planning document, as approved by the general membership of the United States Catholic Conference in November 1985, the Department of Education was authorized to continue its Christian Adulthood Catechetical Resource Book. This current publication, *1987 Christian Adulthood: A Catechetical Resource,* has been prepared by Mr. Neil A. Parent, the Representative for Adult Education, approved by Rev. Thomas G. Gallagher, Secretary of Education, and authorized for publication by the undersigned.

February 19, 1987

Monsignor Daniel F. Hoye
General Secretary
NCCB/USCC

Scriptural excerpts in this book are from *The New American Bible,* copyright © 1970, Confraternity of Christian Doctrine, Washington, D.C., and are used with the permission of the copyright owner.

Excerpts from *Will Our Children Have Faith?* (pp. 94, 97) by John H. Westerhoff III. Copyright © 1976 by The Seabury Press, Inc. Reprinted by permission of Harper & Row Publishers, Inc.

Excerpts from *Family Enrichment with Family Clustering* by Margaret Sawin. Copyright © 1979 by Judson Press, Valley Forge, Pa. Used by permission of Judson Press.

Selection from *What We Have Seen and Heard,* A Pastoral Letter on Evangelization from the Black Bishops of the United States. Copyright © 1984 by St. Anthony Messenger Press, 1615 Republic Street, Cincinnati, OH 45210. All rights reserved.

ISBN 1-55586-106-7

CONTENTS

INTRODUCTION

This marks the fifth volume of *Christian Adulthood*, an annual publication that began in 1982. Added as a special feature of this volume are indices that will enable readers to identify quickly both topics and authors that have appeared in *Christian Adulthood* since its inception. Jane Beno, Seattle, prepared the indices, and we are grateful to her for them.

While the basic format of *Christian Adulthood* has remained constant for the series—specifically, the four-part breakdown of articles into Theoretical Foundations, Program Development, Leadership and Professional Development, and Resources—we have gradually introduced changes designed to assist the reader. For example, we have changed from a double column layout to a single column with wide margins. This was done not only for better eye appeal but also to facilitate easy placement of notes and other reference material on the same page as the text. We also began using photographs of various adult education scenes. These help give visual support to some of the content material and serve to point out the variety of adult education experiences that are occurring around the country. We are pleased that many diocesan offices have been so helpful in supplying us with photographs of their adult education events.

In each volume of *Christian Adulthood*, we have tried to offer a helpful combination of theory and practice. We sought not only to expand the boundaries of theory, but also to provide the kind of practical help that is continually sought by those who are responsible for delivering adult religious education services.

Examples of this twofold purpose in the present volume are articles by Robert Hater and Matthew Hayes. In the Theoretical Foundations section, Hater examines some of the prevailing practices of so-called conversion processes. He notes problems with the wholesale adoption of such practices and offers several principles for what he considers to be a proper and effective approach to facilitating conversion. In the Program Development section, Hayes evaluates some of the more common approaches to learning needs assessment and describes in detail a method that he feels is not only more realistic but more effective as well.

Two main topical areas in this volume are those of family and the RCIA. In James DeBoy's article "Who Is Responsible for Adult Religious Education?" the family plays an important role in shaping adult religious education in a parish. Thomas Lynch, a specialist in family systems, offers some observations about the important implications for family that are part of many an adult education program. And, in the Resources section, Joseph Crisafulli provides a helpful overview of Family Clusters, an intergenerational approach to adult education that has gained notable attention and success both here and abroad.

Regarding the RCIA, Robert Hater questions the wisdom of stressing a singular approach to the catechumenate process; Greer Gordon examines, from an adult learning perspective, the RCIA for the black Catholic; Jacqueline McMakin and Rhoda Nary offer suggestions for building on the RCIA and renewal processes; and Eleanor Rae shares some research data on regional-based approaches to the RCIA.

The remaining articles, each in its own way, offer helpful theory and practice for carrying out an effective adult education ministry.

Neil A. Parent
Representative for Adult Education
Department of Education
United States Catholic Conference

I. THEORETICAL FOUNDATIONS

Introduction

Today, *communidades de base*, the Rite of Christian Initiation of Adults, RENEW, and Shared Christian Praxis are well known to many pastoral ministers. In some way, each pertains to conversion. This article looks at conversion as it relates to methods that facilitate the conversion process.

Evangelization, conversion, and personal growth are treated first, with special reference to three modes of God's revealing presence. Next, conversion and community building are discussed in relation to *communidades de base* and United States culture. The final section considers conversion processes and methodology.

This is no "how-to" article. Its purpose is to present basic philosophical, theological, sociological, and psychological assumptions that can illuminate pastoral ministers in their efforts to facilitate conversion. Its central thesis is that any method used to facilitate conversion must enable people to connect their lives with the gospel story in an atmosphere of mutual love and support.

Evangelization, Conversion, and Personal Growth

Evangelization begins with God seeking us. This divine quest emerges from within us; it is revealed in community and clarified through reflection. Because God's revealing presence dialogues with all dimensions of life, the entire world speaks sacramentally. Hence, evangelization goes beyond specific ecclesial actions.

Modes of God's Revealing Presence[1]

God's revealing presence happens in different ways. Human awareness is like the top of a wave, receiving direction and impetus from deep within. Although each one of us is whole and undivided, reason allows us to identify three ways that the sacramental world discloses links between us, God, and community. These are the Core, Community, and Consideration Modes.[2] Like a swirl or spiral, they move from an intimate depth, where God radically energizes our spirit (Core), to the outer limit of our consciousness (Consideration). The entire movement flows through group response (Community), where family, friends, and culture help shape attitudes and values.

Core Mode

The Core Mode refers to the deepest dimension of the person, from which human energy ultimately emerges, and where primal urges move us to search for meaning. This wellspring, continually energized by God, roots the meaning system of our lives. Here, we meet God in the form of spiritual energy, creative awareness, and intuitive insight. From this source, questions such as, "Who am I?" and "Why was I born?" emerge. At times, in this realm of mystery, the only adequate answer is silence. Here, the sacred explodes from the ground of creation as God grasps us and invites the response: "Amen!"

Questions emerge spontaneously from the Core Mode and cannot

Facilitating Conversion Processes

Robert J. Hater

Robert J. Hater, Ph.D., is a priest of the Archdiocese of Cincinnati and a professor of Religious Studies at the University of Dayton, specializing in pastoral theology and ministry.

1. The modes considered in this article are not meant to describe exhaustively the conversion process but, rather, to illustrate certain dimensions of God's revealing presence manifested through the sacramental world.

2. These modes are rational constructs that do not exist as such; rather, they are used to point to facets of a person's life.

3

be programmed as we respond to the unpredictable invitations of a radically free God. This mode makes it possible for people of different religious beliefs to identify with the meaning of what is said when someone shares an archetypal story or deep personal experience. Not long ago, this happened at a Hindu-Christian prayer service.[3] When a Christian read a scripture account of Jesus' agony and death, the Hindu holy men wept, feeling deeply the universal meaning of sin, suffering, and death.

Community Mode

The Community Mode describes the situations in which humans interact on a deep level (e.g., family, friends, work, church). In community, we are influenced by the way our particular culture interprets the energies flowing from our Core Mode. Cultural, historical, and confessional beliefs affect the shape and focus of these deep, core energies. Because God chooses when, where, and how to reveal "the holy," mystery grounds community. On the other hand, since God is revealed in time, the community formed from faith in this revelation is experiential and historical. Consequently, believing Christians respond to the Jesus story both from a core depth common to all religious people and from their particular belief that Jesus reveals God's healing, forgiveness, and love.

A group's symbol system reflects common stories and beliefs. So, community members who understand the system's meaning share similar responses to it and are guided by it. Every religious group thus influences the symbolic power of its members' actions, words, and events.

Consideration Mode[4]

When we rationally reflect on our actions and beliefs, we are operating in the Consideration Mode. From a religious viewpoint, this enables us to formulate doctrines and creeds, as well as to understand motives for action. This mode also allows us to pass records on to the next generation, to interpret historical events, and to develop models in science and theology.

Models offer rational explanations for historical and scientific data. An evolutionary model, for example, may offer one explanation for the origin of life. A theological model may help to illuminate a person's faith. An individual, after a significant experience, may likewise probe rationally the motivation behind his or her actions. Reflection of this sort is integral to human learning.

While energies flow among Core, Community, and Consideration Modes, the latter mode becomes significant in our personal conversion to the degree that it illuminates the other modes and meshes with them. Otherwise, reflection is an exercise in problem solving, not mystery probing. The aim of all community conversion efforts, including evangelization, catechesis, and liturgy, is to touch the dimension of mystery at the Core Mode, which is more basic than the intellectual conversion of the Consideration Mode.[5]

These three modes, focusing the divine energies that root evangelization, spiral from deep within us, through community to conscious-

3. This experience was related in a private conversation with Ignatius Hirudayam, SJ. The event took place at a Christian-Hindu prayer service in Madras, South India.

4. The Consideration Mode includes cognitive, affective, and sensory responses.

5. For a more systematic treatment of the relationship between evangelization, catechesis, and liturgy, see Robert J. Hater, *Parish Catechetical Ministry* (Encino, Calif.: Bensiger Publishing Co., 1986).

Diocese of Salinas

ness, only to return again to their source in a constant vortex of human awareness.

Conversion and Community Building

Community is central to God's revealing presence and always conditions it. Thus, knowledge of and sensitivity to society are important for facilitating individual and communal conversion.

Three contemporary movements offer new ways to facilitate the conversion process: *communidades de base*; methodologies aimed at structuring the conversion process; and the Rite of Christian Initiation of Adults. Each movement must address the person's Core Mode. The Core Mode always relates to community (family, friends, neighborhood, church) because personal uniqueness emerges from group response, with communal beliefs and attitudes grounding an individual's growth.

Since the Core Mode is linked with communal action, it is helpful to look at the basic energies operative in community. The patterns that keep a love relationship together, solidify family ties, or ensure healthy work relationships go deeper than rational planning. When people come together, something always happens. At times, this is positive: love, cooperation, and trust; but the opposite also occurs: jealousy, bickering, and destructive competition. Whatever the outcome, the term *mythos* refers to the group's collective, foundational attitude. The group's distinctive response patterns are called *mythical patterns*, which are lived and celebrated in *rituals* (church, family, societal rituals).

Communidades de Base and United States Culture: A Contrast[6]

Every family, friendship, office, parish, or country has a distinct mythos, which establishes the basic groundwork for human interaction.

6. Some helpful insights concerning *comunidades de base* have been taken from a reaction to the first draft of this manuscript by Paul F. Knitter, professor of Theology, Xavier University, Cincinnati, Ohio. His comments are incorporated in this section.

The mythos undergirds a group's story or *myth*, which can be conveyed orally, in writing, or through technology.

The story from which *communidades de base* emerges, reflects small communities that are usually poor, Catholic, and oppressed. Struggling for freedom, they hear and respond to God's Word in a distinctive way. They embody similar mythical patterns that people live out through various ritual responses, such as collective solidarity, opposition to oppressors, and freedom movements.

The myth liberating the poor in Central and South America is more than their cultural myth, aspects of which cause their oppression; it is also their Christian myth, brought alive in their efforts to change political and social conditions.

Clearly, the cultural mythos and ritual responses of Central and South America differ from those in the United States. Consequently, God's evangelizing Word will not be heard in the same way, even though the Christian story or myth is similar everywhere.

Communidades de base teaches us the power of small-group response, where experience is enlightened by the Christian myth, revealed especially in Scripture. When using aspects of this method, however, it is important to realize that our mythical patterns are different from those in Latin America. If the *communidades de base* method is to succeed in the United States, it must help us respond to God's Word in our highly individualistic society, influenced by frontier freedom and a functional world view.

Small-group sharing is not new in the Catholic Church in the United States. Over the years, effective teachers, the Christian Family Movement, Sodality, retreats, cell movements, Young Christian Students, and others have used this method. However, the use of Scripture to illuminate experience is a special contribution of *communidades de base* to the Catholic community. This approach, only minimally emphasized before Vatican II, is now central to contemporary catechesis.

However, to impose without modification a method that is effective in one setting (Latin America) on a different one (United States) may net limited results. In *communidades de base*, people assemble in natural settings, such as small villages with close family and neighborhood ties. They share from a deeply bonded experience, one linked by common needs or oppression. By contrast, American neighborhoods, parishes, and families are quite different. Neighborhoods are usually heterogeneous; parishes are comprised of members with various personal, professional, and ethnical backgrounds; and, the family is very diverse in its makeup: nuclear, single-parent, childless, divorced, and blended. With fewer cultural and religious bonds, it makes it harder for Catholics in this country to link on an ultimate level.

In the United States, when we meet to share in parish or school groups, the results may be functional, random, and superficial. After a parish group session, some of us may never associate again because we have little daily contact, and even less long-term bonding and commitment. Infrequent personal association makes communication and trust difficult.

In our country, natural groups exist in family, workplaces, senior citizen complexes, schools, sports activities, support groups, clubs, and various organizations. We need to acknowledge such natural groups as offering rich possibilities for using the basic dynamism of *communidades de base*. These natural groups point to unique features of the United States experience, involving high mobility, freedom, individualism, and a rational outlook. They also hint at why church functions are often sparsely attended—the people's mythos is not in tune with the parish leaders' attempts to "gather the folks."

Today, a curious phenomenon surfaces in our highly functional society. The individual, rational, and mobile dynamism motivating us seems to be turning back upon itself and causing us to reexamine our roots.[7] Can we live for long in a functional world without searching for ultimate meaning? From deep within our collective awareness, a search for wholeness, intimacy, and meaning emerges. This points to a new mysticism, which strives for connections rooted in the need for deep relationships. Here, causally unrelated events often become the stuff of life, such as when Jim is introduced to Beth and they fall in love and marry; or, when two families meet at a Little League event, become friends, and subsequently support each other in joy and tragedy. As events like these happen, people yearn for happiness, love, and shared rituals.

If parishes help people connect at the Core Mode in order to meet the anguish of a spiritually starved generation, Church, family, and workplace become dialogue partners, revealing the already-present God.[8] This happens best when church leaders are sensitive to the dynamics of American culture.

At the same time, the *communidades de base* experience contains important insights. The structure and method of the base communities include more than meeting in small groups and interpreting Scripture in light of concrete experiences. People also try to specify the kind of experience that most illuminates God's Word. They ask what kind of experience best clears away the ideologies and smoke screens that prevent them from hearing what God is saying to them. That experience is primarily one of oppression in its various forms. Only by getting in touch with the experience of being oppressed or of being part of a system that oppresses, thereby producing nonpersons (poor), can they truly hear the fullness of what God intends to reveal through Jesus, his Gospel, and his Church.[9]

The issue of oppression might be one way to apply the base Christian community method to the United States. Perhaps, it is a way of forming, then providing, some stability for small groups within a larger parish population. If we share our experiences of being both oppressed and oppressors, we can hear God's Word anew and be drawn back into community.

If we use the *communidades de base* method, the "base" must include the dialogue of family, work, and Church in order to allow the authentic myth of the group to emerge. Otherwise, the method will be incomplete and artificially imposed. Today, we search for new ways to discover community within our cultural context.

7. See Robert Bellah, *Habits of the Heart* (Berkeley: University of California Press, 1985).

8. See Robert J. Hater, "Evangelization and the Priesthood of All Believers," *Evangelizing Adults,* Glenn C. Smith, ed. (Wheaton, Ill.: Tyndale House Publishers, 1985), pp. 66–70.

9. To appreciate Jesus' teaching on the poor (nonperson), it is important to stress continually the Kingdom theme of the Gospels. The term *nonperson* refers to the situation where an individual, because of a cultural or personal condition, finds it difficult or impossible to achieve the goal of becoming a free, integral human being.

United States Cultural Characteristics: Implications for Community Building

North American culture offers unique characteristics that can be integrated into ways of becoming community. These characteristics flow from our history as a racially mixed, free people who still have a frontier spirit and are highly influenced by science and technology. There are three unique characteristics of our culture that can reveal distinctive dimensions of God's presence: plurality, individuality, and mobility.

Plurality and freedom are cherished values in this country. From colonial days, various ethnic peoples arrived here hoping for freedom's dream. The ensuing mix formed a cultural pattern unique in world history. With this came distinctive life styles, challenges, and ways to approach issues.

We are sensitive to personal rights and responsibilities, especially in family and workplace. Freedom is jealously guarded and personhood affirmed. For this reason, community in the Catholic Church in the United States is unique, for we ground our church community mythos in the cultural mythos that formed us.

Free people react differently from those in totalitarian countries or even from those highly influenced by traditional ethnic values. This is evident in the ways various cultures deal with conflict or dissent. North American culture accepts different viewpoints and dissent as the right of free people. The freedom to disagree grounds our cultural reality; yet, it does not threaten the basic fiber of our culture. By contrast, nondemocratic institutions often see conflict, divergent views, and dissent as challenging culture itself.

Today, many of us Catholics in the United States sense God's presence in the freedom we cherish. While remaining faithful to the Church, we struggle to form our consciences in a mature, responsible way, rooting our decisions in the freedom deeply embedded in our culture.

Individuality goes hand-in-hand with freedom. Free people are individuals who discover life's meaning in communities that respect their rights. Often, while stressing community, church people play down individuality as presenting a barrier to common interests. Seen negatively, individuality means that the person is concerned for oneself, with little regard for others. But, is this generally true of our citizens? To be sure, we cherish individuality, but are we not also a generous people? Individuality, indeed, can foster generosity, love, and compassion.

As Catholics in the United States, we cherish individuality and, thus, gain insight into our personal uniqueness before God. A free God creates a free people made in the divine image. Our individuality helps us discover our uniqueness before God, and how God gives different gifts to different people.

Individuality is a given for us. It is a cultural starting point that affirms the specialness of everyone. Beginning here, the Church can help participants affirm their natural communities and move to deeper modes of personal (Core Mode) and communal (Community Mode) conversion.

From earliest times, we in the United States have been on the move.

Impelled by a frontier spirit, we have migrated from coastal regions to plains, mountains, and deserts. And, our expansion continues into the new frontiers of space and ocean.

This mobility discloses another face of God. The Christian God is an active God. Also, we are a "Pilgrim People," always in process, needing fulfillment. In a mobile world, we are called to discover a deeper, more permanent intimacy with God (Core Mode). When this happens, we are graced to discover a new kind of intimacy with people.

Some people stress the negative side of mobility. But, it is part of who we are. It would be hard to live without the kind of mobility made possible by automobiles, buses, or airplanes. Mobility has rearranged our life styles and shifted our support systems from extended family and neighbors to a country-wide network of family colleagues, friends, and interest groups. Mobility allows families to be supported by people beyond the immediate family group.

Mobility poses a special challenge to church communities. Some parishes have a high parishioner turnover rate. In this setting, long-term intimacy is difficult, making it important to encourage parishioners to identify the Core Mode of their lives, so that the intimacy discovered there can flow to others. In a highly mobile society, the church that identifies family and marketplace (work associates, friends, natural support groups) as places where God is especially present, does a great service to its parishioners.

Communidades de Base and United States Culture:
Pastoral Conclusions

After analyzing *communidades de base* and unique characteristics of United States culture, certain pastoral conclusions are suggested.

1. The cultural myths and rituals of Latin America and the United States are different. This has to be considered in any effort to apply the *communidades de base* method to our experience.
2. The core myth of Christianity is the same for all people. It centers around God's universal love, revealed especially in the biblical teaching on the Kingdom of God. Here, we discover God's preferential option for the nonperson (poor).
3. Scripture reading is an integral part of *communidades de base*. The Christian story helps illuminate a cultural situation as people reflect upon their experience. Pastorally, the Christian story can always shed new light on personal or community experience.
4. By adapting *communidades de base* methods, our social or community experience can be also clarified. For example, we can identify the ways in which we suffer or cause others to suffer and discern how we might address these issues. Such sharing of individual or community experiences, in light of our Catholic Christian story, can help solidify a group.
5. The Christian myth (stressing God's love for the nonperson) and the cultural myth (disclosing both God's presence and the how, when, and where of oppression) invite people to the Core and

Community Modes, where deep conversion happens. In this process, rational reflection is valuable when it allows people to hear and respond more fully to God's evangelizing activities.

6. The unique characteristics of United States culture, especially plurality, individuality, and mobility, ground our cultural and church mythos. Church efforts to address pastoral concerns, including conversion processes, need to root the Christian myth in our society.

Conversion Processes

Since Vatican II, many methods aimed at facilitating conversion, have developed in the Catholic Church. These include the Rite of Christian Initiation of Adults, RENEW, Christ Renews His Parish, Marriage Encounter, Cursillo, and Shared Christian Praxis.

Conversion, Conversion Processes, and Methodology

Conversion is understood as a significant deepening, recentering, or refocusing of life patterns, energy, and loyalties, as well as a shift or deepening of attitudes or values. It is a process that can be either individual or communal.

Rooted in the human depths (Core Mode), individual conversion happens in and through community, for all life involves human interaction. Communal conversion, in turn, is rooted in the mythos and rituals of the group (Community Mode) and happens largely through forces operative in the collective unconscious.

A distinction must be made between the conversion process itself, which always happens in a person or group, and methods used to facilitate it.[10] The former is an end; the latter are means. The ultimate purpose of individual or communal conversion is deeper union with God, achieved through relationships with the sacramental word. Every effort to facilitate conversion (e.g., evangelization, catechesis, group sharing, liturgical celebrations) is a method or learning process involving a person and an environment.

The person brings to the environment a certain mythos resulting from past experiences. The environment, having its own mythos, can be private space (e.g., retreat, solitary walk in the woods, privacy of one's room) or group interaction (family, friends, work, church events).

Four elements are common to the Christian conversion process: (1) personal experience; (2) that experience encountering a broader environment, including the larger Christian story; (3) illuminating the experience through the encounter and grounding it in prayer, Scripture, church teaching, and history; (4) responding to the insights gleaned in acts of prayer, service, and celebration. These four elements need not flow sequentially or be present at all times, and, each element can happen whether one is alone or with others.

The above description of the conversion process is a theoretical construct pointing to central elements in the actual movement of conversion. Within this context, various conversion methods are developed, applied,

10. The term *method* or *methodology* is used in a broad sense to refer to any process intended to help facilitate individual or communal conversion.

and evaluated. A method is valuable if it helps a person to discover God present within experience and to reflect upon life in light of the Christian story, so as to move toward some type of life-style response, such as repentance, prayer, social action, or charity.

Methods vary from lectures (generally teacher-centered) to dialogue (learner-centered). Different methods can be used at different phases of the conversion process. Effective methods take into account the mythos of both the person and the environment and the facilitator's gifts. There is no one best method to facilitate conversion or learning.

The distinction between the conversion process, itself, and the various methods used to facilitate it is critical. For example, the Rite of Christian Initiation of Adults advocates a flexible process, accommodated to personal needs and local circumstances.[11] In other words, conversion is central. How it is fostered is a question of methodology. When this distinction is not clear, problems arise, especially if the rite, itself, or a particular way of doing it is canonized.

Several examples illustrate this. One happened at a RCIA workshop. A participant became disturbed when a leader advised her to send a catechumen to another parish if that person were unwilling to join the parish catechumenal group. Today, the ordinary way of fostering ecclesial conversion is through a catechumenal group; but, opportunities for participating in a modified catechumenate, including private instructions, also have to be provided. This is a question of methodology. The goal is conversion, which can happen with or without the ordinary parish catechumenal process.

A second example happened at another RCIA workshop. Here, the leader insisted that the only way to catechise in the catechumenate is to use exclusively the readings from the lectionary; no other books should be used. Who says so? The origins of the catechumenate reveal different methodologies developed in various churches (Rome, Jerusalem, Hippo, Constantinople, Milan) to prepare catechumens.[12] A statement like this absolutizes a method, which is only a means to help facilitate conversion.

A final example pertains to catechetical processes. One catechetical process used today employs a procedure that always begins with some kind of participant sharing. To say that group sharing must happen first in every instance is just as problematic as to insist that a lecture or storytelling always must precede group sharing. Whenever a method to facilitate conversion is absolutized, as often happened with the pre-Vatican II catechism method, the complexity of a person's conversion process can be lost. The method, then, may become more important than the person.

Many Methods To Facilitate Conversion

Any systematic attempt to help facilitate the conversion process must consider four factors: person(s), context, method (including content materials), and facilitator. The method chosen in any structured conversion situation should address these factors, centering around the mythical dimensions involved.

Conversion differs from person to person. Someone may wish to

11. See the *Rite of Christian Initiation of Adults,* nos. 1–5. Unfortunately, certain rather dogmatic assertions proposed today—the best or only way to catechize within the RCIA or other aspects of this process—seem to go contrary to the flexibility required by the RCIA. In stating that the RCIA is a method, this author presumes that it is a process, not a program.

12. No universally accepted pattern of catechetical methodology is evident in the early history of the catechumenate. As the catechumenate developed, the Sunday Liturgy of the Word played a primary, but not exclusive, part in the content of catechetical instructions. In addition, catechetical and formational experiences sometimes happened in conjunction with the Liturgy of the Hours or at other times, often emphasizing the creed (see Augustine and Egeria, below). Most local churches followed a manner of instruction that shifted focus as catechumens moved from the initial stage of becoming catechumens, through the time immediately preceding baptism, to postbaptismal catechesis. The method of catechesis was not the same in all churches. Instructions varied in approach and focus, apparently adapted to the bishop, ministers, place, and people. Augustine (Hippo) seemingly aimed at eliciting a simple response of initial belief from the inquirer but stressed the importance of instruction in the creed for catechumens (see Augustine, *The First Catechetical Instruction,* Ancient Christian Writers [Washington, D.C.: Newman Press, 1946]). In the early churches, the content of catechumenal instructions seemed to fall into two main categories. Catechesis, like that of Ambrose (Milan) and Cyril (Jerusalem), emphasized explaining the Scriptures, faith, and creed (see Ambrose, *De Abraham:* Cyril, *Protocatechesis*). In Jerusalem, instructions followed this format and included much more than explaining the Sunday readings; Ambrose and Cyril interpreted the meaning of the sacraments for the neophytes soon after baptism (see Egeria, in J. Wilkerson, *Egeria's Travels* [London: SPCK, 1971]). Chrysostom (Constantinople), by contrast, followed no systematic form of catechesis; he was concerned with faith and action, morality and virtue. Catechumens were instructed, in detail, about baptismal ceremonies before baptism (see Chrysos-

11

spend time alone to enhance conversion. Later, he or she may prefer limited group interaction or more intense dialogue. The person's mythos significantly determines the most appropriate method.

Selecting a method depends on the mythical perspective or context of the people. In one instance, it may be wise to begin with a dialogue; in another, with a didactic approach, gradually moving to a collaborative one. No one method works at all times with all people.

Because the individual's mythos significantly influences the conversion process, methodology and content materials should touch the mythical perspectives of the person or group. People's divergent mythical attitudes also indicate why any systematic approach to conversion needs to move beyond the Community and Consideration Modes to the Core Mode.

The facilitator's style will influence the method used. Some people are good group facilitators; others are more successful using a modified lecture format. To require all facilitators, such as catechists, group coordinators, and teachers to adhere to the same technique is akin to believing that all learners come from the same mythical perspective. For example, not all religion teachers or catechists can use the same method or textbook. In addition, not all RCIA processes need to employ the same method. If a method works for one group and facilitator, leading people to a deeper faith awareness, a better appreciation of community, and a more profound link with God, who can say that another method would be better? The bottom line is conversion, not method.

Facilitating Conversion Processes

Conversion helps us gain insight into life's meaning. Consequently, efforts to facilitate conversion center around shared meaning. In a sacramental, incarnational world, the search for meaning always returns to the Core Mode, where God intimately addresses us. Our relationship with God roots all shared meaning, is the goal of conversion, and is enhanced by dialogue. Thus, to facilitate conversion is to acknowledge the mythos out of which we respond.

The world within which God invites us to new levels of awareness includes three chief disclosure points: family, ecclesial community, and personal activities (work, prayer, play, friends, community involvement, nature).

Facilitating conversion means acknowledging these disclosure points in our culture, seeing God's presence there, and developing methodologies consistent with the heterogeneous mix of our learners. Specifically, this implies appreciating the unique characteristics of plurality, individuality, and mobility as well as the insights gleaned from mythically different population groups, such as *communidades de base*. In this context, it helps to distinguish natural groups (e.g., separated and divorced people, children who lost a parent) from more random groups (e.g., youth catechetical group, adult enrichment program). A common concern binds together natural groups; random groups usually do not have the same binding force.

This does not mean that there is no central focus for the conversion

tom, *Baptismal Instructions,* Ancient Christian Writers [Westminster, Md.: Newman Press, 1963]). These different methods become evident in the varying approaches taken to mystagogical catechesis by Ambrose and Cyril on the one hand and by Chrysostom on the other (see Chrysostom, *op. cit.,* and Ambrose, *On the Sacraments and On the Mysteries* [London: SPCK,1950]). Historical data confirms the need to remain flexible in both content and method used in the RCIA (helpful research data supplied by General Kramer, OP, Athenaeum of Ohio).

process. There is one common center toward which all conversion processes converge and around which all methodologies focus. This common center, touching the Core Mode, is every person's search for meaning and God, in the midst of a common oppression, rooted in sin and imperfection and pointing to a world in need of healing. This search for meaning and common experience of oppression, of being at times a nonperson, reveals why Jesus' life and ministry focused on the poor—the nonpersons of this world. In Jesus' teaching, poverty (economic, psychological, physical, spiritual) is an evil to be overcome; the nonperson (poor) is God's special concern.[13] What person does not experience some form of poverty? This common bonding of poor people provides the starting point for all efforts to facilitate conversion, efforts that ultimately focus at the Core Mode, where God alone can make a person whole.

In the United States, our highly individualized, scientific, technological, and pragmatic outlook can easily allow us to neglect the Core Mode by stressing a functional world view that implies that anything not measurable is second-rate or meaningless. In this context, methods to facilitate conversion must move beyond the functional to address ultimate questions.

Community is central to conversion. An individual "becomes" in community, which begins with the family. Martin Buber said that it takes a "Thou" to create an "I."[14] In community, God is disclosed; in community, a person is supported and encouraged; in community, personal meaning is most fully revealed. Because community influence differs with each person, individuals interpret a communal mythos differently. Acknowledging unity in diversity, yet diversity in community, reinforces the need for flexible methodologies, as people move across the boundaries of age, group, parish, and country. While Core Mode questions are the same for all people, the mythical responses in community vary greatly due to local circumstances and group differences. Although needing community, personal conversion is always an individual search and ought to be facilitated as such.

The Consideration Mode allows people to articulate meaning in a systematic way. Intuition is rooted in the Core Mode, rational reflection in the Consideration Mode. These modes are intellectual constructs, not existing in themselves apart from the totality of the person. Intuitive, cognitive, affective, and sensory responses are aspects of one process. It is important to emphasize their interplay, otherwise, subjectivity and objectivity can become artificially dichotomized. This is especially true when looking for methods to facilitate the conversion process. By using adequate methodologies, the conversion process can move to a level deeper than rational reflection, although the latter is important to clarify feelings, test intuitions, analyze situations, and probe scripture and church history.

The goal of a systematic effort to facilitate conversion is to deepen a person's relationship with God by blending Core, Community, and Consideration Modes into a viable synthesis. To accomplish this, several questions should be asked:

1. Do the efforts to facilitate conversion recognize the difference

13. The Scriptures help us appreciate the difference between *poverty* and *the poor*. See also, 1971 Synod of Bishops' document *Justice in the World* [Washington, D.C.: USCC Office of Publishing and Promotion Services, 1971], pp. 33–34.
14. See Martin Buber, *I and Thou* (New York: Charles Scribner's Sons, 1970).

between the conversion process itself, which is lifelong, and the various methods intended to help facilitate aspects of this process?

2. Does the method stress the Core Mode, while addressing the needs of the whole person? To emphasize the cognitive, affective, or sensory realms, without integrating them, is inadequate. God's evangelizing action happens in the whole person—body, emotions, mind, and spirit. If a method hopes to touch the Core Mode, it must take into account the oneness of the person.

3. Is it best to start a structured effort to facilitate the conversion process by using a method that begins with personal sharing, or is it preferable to start with the larger story or aspects of it and then to connect people's individual experiences with the common story? This question has no simple answer. It depends on the situation, time, facilitator, and mythos of the group. There is not one method for all occasions. Each group and facilitator needs to be considered before deciding the best method to use.

4. Is the method adequate, considering the age of the people with whom it is used? The attention span of small children differs from that of adults. Children learn rituals; adolescents and adults search for the meaning of rituals and life. Adults have a rich font of experience; children do not. A method that works well with one age group may not be as effective with people of another age.

5. Does the method used to facilitate conversion provide a base where the individual or group mythos can be developed, challenged, or motivated to action and from which a new myth can emerge? Renewal movements, such as Cursillo and Charismatic groups, attempt to do this by connecting persons to a larger community and providing support or nourishment for their life actions.

6. When necessary, can the method challenge the mythos of the United States, of the Church, or of other social groups? At times, a method emphasizing human rights and responsibilities can challenge seriously civil and church authority to reflect on how well a particular group incorporates the charity and justice demands of the Scriptures.

7. How does the method try to inculturate a myth that is transcultural? Some conversion methods may address this question by stressing the participants' personal freedom and inculturation; others may stress following the teachings of ecclesial authority.

Parishes, schools, and various community groups need flexibility in order to channel the power of the mythos within which people live. This requires developing a sensitivity to different age and personality groups, as well as considering the personal, family, peer, church, work, and ethnic factors influencing an individual. When this happens, evangelization becomes sacramental, and God's Word bears fruit.

Conclusion

Today's complex world invites Christians to return to the simple message of the Gospels and to evangelize in a holistic way. In our culture, this means recognizing the diversity of people and being realistic about community in our time. To proclaim the Good News, no one methodology is sufficient. Rather, Christian ministers must respond to personal and group needs and look again at how Jesus taught—by sharing a message, telling a story, inviting people to come together to consider its consequences and derive meaning from the mystery of God-among-us. Jesus gave this challenge to his first disciples; he also gives it to us.

The Spirituality of the Black Catholic Adult

Greer G. Gordon

Greer G. Gordon is former assistant director of Adult Religious Education/ Formation in the Archdiocese of Washington and a member of the Carmelite Community, Baltimore, Maryland.

Introduction

Volumes have been written on the subject of Catholic spirituality from the perspective of the broader community. Precious little, however, has been developed on this subject from the perspective of the black believer. Although much of what will be presented here could be said of all Catholics, it is my intention to unfold some aspects of the spiritual tradition of the Catholic Church from the black perspective.

The Context

With the close of the Second Vatican Council, the Church embarked upon the arduous journey of *aggiornamento*. The council Fathers encouraged Holy Mother Church not only to retain the wisdom and richness of the past but also to greet the needs of the future with clarity and a renewed vision. In essence, the Church was called to reexamine her identity in the modern world. This quest necessarily led the Church to a more critical investigation of the cultural, historical, and philosophical influences that, for better or worse, had radically impacted upon her development and formation. For example: liturgists returned to an investigation of the writings of the early Fathers and the early forms of worship; religious communities rediscovered their primitive constitutions and with them the spirit of their founders and foundresses; members of the black and Hispanic communities addressed the need for the freedom to express the richness of their own cultures in and through liturgy and catechetics. This process of *aggiornamento* has summoned us to a deeper understanding of who we are and who we are called to be as a people dedicated to God.

One of the by-products of the council has been a resurgence of interest in the meaning of Catholic spirituality. The Catholic Church in the United States, over the past fifteen years, has experienced a notable renaissance of spiritual writing, which has focused upon the communal and individual aspects of our relationship with God. This climate of reflective evaluation, along with a host of socioeconomic and cultural influences, has given rise to the black Catholic community's affirmation of the wisdom and richness of our heritage. In their pastoral letter *What We Have Seen and Heard*, the black bishops of the United States state:

> There is a richness of our Black experience that we must share with the entire People of God. These are gifts that are part of an African past. For we have heard with Black ears and we have seen with Black eyes and we have understood with an African heart. We thank God for the gifts of our Catholic faith and we give thanks for the gifts of our Blackness. In all humility we turn to the whole Church that it might share our gifts so that "our joy may be complete" (p. 4).

Like the broader Church, the black Catholic community has begun the process of seriously reflecting upon our identity. As we have asked the question, "What does it mean to be black and Catholic?"; we have also had to ask, "What is our relationship to our non-Catholic black brothers and sisters?"

An Unnecessary Apologia

Black Catholics in the United States comprise a very small percentage of the total population of black believers. The vast majority of black people would appear to be members of more "Word-oriented" Christian communities, such as the Baptist and Pentecostal Churches. The Catholic Church is a more "table-oriented" faith. Although the Word is an integral part of the celebration, the Eucharist is the central focus of the worship service. Thus, the Catholic worship service focuses not only upon the celebration of the Word but also upon the celebration of the table. It is for this reason that the order of the Mass is divided into the Liturgy of the Word and the Liturgy of the Eucharist. It is important to remember that the Catholic faith is grounded in Scripture and tradition. This is a notable difference from some of our Protestant brothers and sisters. Many Catholics, when attempting to dialogue with non-Catholic Christians, oftentimes confusedly present the Catholic faith as being grounded in simply tradition or Scripture. The unity of Scripture and tradition must be recalled with care and clarity.

The centrality of the Eucharist is a key component of Catholic spirituality. The inability of many black Catholics to articulate clearly the differences between the Catholic faith and some Protestant faiths oftentimes leads them to feel the need to defend their reasons for being a black person who is a member of the Catholic community. Many black people would have us believe that "black spirituality" means "black Protestant spirituality." Thus, black Catholics frequently have found the need to give an apologia or defense of their Catholicism. This is unnecessary.

For, as a people, we recall with pain the suffering of our ancestors who lived in bondage and chains. As a people, we recall with disdain the racism that made it impossible for us to drink from an undesignated water fountain. As a people, we recall and continue to live with the subtle forms of prejudice that deny black people the gift of a positive self-image, an image that, in fact, is created by God. As a people, we recall with all Jewish and Christian believers the fact that God brought the children of Israel out of bondage and into the Promised Land. As a people, we recall with all Christians the fact that God has freed us from the bondage of sin, in and through the death and resurrection of his only begotten Son. The Eucharist is the celebration of our salvation in Christ. Is it, then, not most appropriate that we, as black people, gather around that table?

When black Catholics gather around the table of sacrifice, we bring with us our corporate identity as well as our individual identities. We bring before the table of the Lord the pain, the suffering, and the struggle that have been ours. Yet, we do so in faith, knowing that our God is a compassionate and merciful God. In the very fiber of our being, we proclaim and celebrate the fact that "the Lord is my life and my salvation . . . whom shall I fear?"

A Unique Way of Knowing and Relating

The black person's corporate and individual recollections of pain and sorrow unite him in a deeply sensing way to the celebration of the Eucharist, the very celebration that unites all Catholic believers in the Church universal. Yet, in the unity of our Catholic worship there is diversity. The need for cultural expression within liturgical celebrations is not a sign of disunity but, rather, a sign of healthy diversity within the unity of the Church. The music, movement, and preaching styles within the black Catholic community carry a sense of the passionate longing for, and delight in, the presence of the Lord. Many black people themselves cannot articulate why they feel this need. They only know that it comes from the very depths of their hearts and that it must be expressed.

Perhaps, it would be helpful to reflect upon why black people express their faith in this fashion. In other words, what is there within the corporate identity of black people that inclines them toward a more passionately expressive way of knowing and relating to God and to the community of faith? Fundamentally, this is an epistemological question, a question of how black people come to know, understand, and relate to the reality that is around them.

Unfortunately, there have been very few, if any, attempts at addressing the epistemological differences that may exist among various cultures. Although it is not possible to enter into such a discussion at this time, it is helpful to note that black psychologists have suggested that black people, as a whole, appear to be highly intuitive and emotive in their ways of knowing and relating. That is, that they tend to perceive and respond to the realities around them in and through the powers of intuition and emotion. This offers a tremendous insight into the spirituality of the black Catholic community. For, if spirituality is understood as being the believer's quest or search for God and how that believer practices the ideals of the life of the Spirit, then it is important for the individual to understand how he or she perceives and relates to God. Out of a posture of increased self-knowledge, it is possible for the individual to continue the journey toward God.

An Intuitive Way of Knowing

Intuition is a way of knowing, a way of perceiving and unfolding reality. In terms of the spiritual life, intuition can be spoken of as an interior sensing, a hope-filled visioning, or the knowledge of the heart. In and through the power of intuition, the black person comes to know who his God is and who he or she is in relationship to God and others.

Black believers have always intuited the presence of God. Deep within themselves, the black people come to know, without really understanding, that there is that which is totally beyond themselves: the source of all life, goodness, and truth. Although this power is known, there really is not a need to comprehend it fully. All that is necessary are the consoling thoughts of the black spiritual: ". . . never alone; I don't have to worry 'cause I'm never alone. He walks beside me every day. He guides my footsteps along the way. Never alone; I don't have to worry 'cause I'm never alone." Yes, like his ancestors, he knows that it is the Lord, who guides and directs his life.

The Scriptures tell us that the person who is in God's favor "walks with God." The Book of Genesis states that Adam (prior to his fall) as well as Enoch and Noah walked with God. The concept of walking with God conveys the notion of constant presence, which can only be experienced within the interior life of the person. This interior knowledge of the presence of the Lord can, if developed, give rise to a life posture of unceasing prayer. How many of us have heard our elders quietly utter: "Lord have mercy"; "stay with me, Jesus"; or "Lord give me strength"? This is, in fact, an example of what St. Paul meant by "pray always." The practice of unceasing prayer, constant presence before the Lord, leads one to a contemplative stance, to which all believers are called, in and through their baptism.

This does not mean that the person is constantly in Church or constantly praying in a formal way. It means that the individual is aware of the fact that God is near. In a brief and quiet moment unknown to anyone else, the believer speaks with and listens to the Lord. It is within the very heart that the Lord knows the believer and the believer knows the Lord. That is, in classical terms, the knowledge of the heart. It would appear that the intuitive personality, with its gift of interior sensing, has an increased tendency toward the development of this type of prayer.

Thus, it would appear that black people are far more gifted by God than they may even realize; for the Lord has blessed them with a fundamental tendency toward the interior life. This most assuredly leads them to the very core of Catholic spirituality, allowing them the possibility of walking along similar paths of such spiritual mothers and fathers of faith as Cyprian, Anthony of Egypt, John Cassian, Benedict of Nursia, Moses the Black, Bernard of Clairveaux, Francis of Assisi, Benedict the Black, Gertrude, Teresa of Avila, John of the Cross, Martin de Porres, Therese of Lisieux, Elizabeth Lange, Henriette Delille, Elizabeth Seton, John Neuman, Thomas Merton, and Dorothy Day.

This gifted interior sensing is the basis of the hope-filled visioning that has made it possible for generations upon generations of believers to survive the worst forms of inhumanity and injustice. For, all that was truly necessary was the heartfelt knowledge of God, that total and complete reliance upon the Lord.

In the process of coming to know the Lord, the believer comes to understand and affirm that he or she is a person of worth, a person of value, who is formed in the image and likeness of God. From this naturally flows the ability to relate with and express an appreciation of others. This fundamental movement toward the formation of community thrusts the believer into the heart of the worshiping assembly, which provides the forum out of which the believer expresses with others his or her deep and abiding dependence upon God.

An Emotive Way of Relating

Emotion is a way of relating, a way of expressing and responding to that which is perceived. In terms of the Spiritual Life, emotion can be spoken of as being a single-hearted or conviction-filled response. It is the response of the "passionate heart." In and through the power of emotion, black people respond to the knowledge they have gained of God, themselves, and others.

The believer's emotive way of relating is clearly heard in the prophet Jeremiah's outcry to the Lord:

You duped me, O Lord, and I let myself be duped;
   you were too strong for me, and you triumphed.
All the day I am an object of laughter;
   everyone mocks me.
Whenever I speak, I must cry out . . .
I say to myself, I will not mention him,
   I will speak in his name no more.
But then it becomes like a fire burning
   in my heart, imprisoned in my bones;
I grow weary holding it in . . . (Jer 20:7–8a,9).

The emotive believer knows that one *cannot not* express passionate love of and commitment to the Lord. The passionate heart must be free to express not only belief in God but also the momentary doubts about one's own ability to share the Good News. This is why we gather with other believers; for, we can only be supported in the living out of our faith by those who are also seeking our God. The recitation of the creed during the worship service is not a statement to the unbelieving world but, rather, a recollective affirmation of who we say we are as followers of Christ.

Thus, conviction-filled, passionate-hearted black believers are thrust into the core of the Church's mission of evangelization. They are by their very nature called to share the Good News of Jesus Christ. Like Jeremiah, they may at times feel that they have been duped, but coupled with their deeply sensing knowledge of God, they will again and again choose to speak the word of the Lord. Black people are, as such, staunchly un-waivering believers.

Developing the Gifts

To paraphrase St. Teresa of Avila, "to whom much is given, much is expected." The Lord has given us two extraordinary gifts, and this is not to speak of what he has given each of us as individuals. These gifts must be developed and placed at the service of the Church. For, they are two of the ingredients of our process of moving more deeply into a relationship with God. This process of conversion, our journey in faith, is nourished by reflection, celebration, and discipline.

Reflection or private prayer is *the* form of communication with God. These moments of stillness provide us with the opportunity to listen and to respond to the Lord. Therefore, prayer is essential to the further development of our relationship with God.

Celebration or public worship is the communal dimension of our relationship with him. We gather, as did the members of the early Church, to give praise and honor to God: "They devoted themselves to the apostles' instruction and the communal life, to the breaking of the bread and the prayers" (Acts 2:42). When we share in the breaking of the bread, the Eucharist, we celebrate the saving deeds of God in Christ. We also acknowledge that we are communal creatures who need to share our faith, our love with others.

Discipline or faithfulness is another essential element of our spiritual lives. Faithfulness draws our attention to the fact that relationships must be nourished by love and care. Our relationship to the Lord cannot become an "on again, off again" experience. Like any relationship, it calls for time to come to know the beloved. It is important to note that the times of both private and communal prayer are entered into regularly. Thus, our journey toward the Lord is composed of all the elements of human growth.

Catechetical Insights

If we make use of our innate gifts, then we must share them with others. We must continue to evangelize and catechize both ourselves and the world. In order to do this, it is necessary to develop and implement (1) strong adult, youth, and children's catechetical programs in our parishes, being certain that we teach not only Scripture but doctrine as well, using methods that are appropriate to the learning styles and developmental processes of each of these groups; (2) the Rite of Christian Initiation of Adults, whereby others may come to understand and enter into this faith community; and (3) programs that help our adults to translate what they know of the faith into the fiber of their daily lives, helping them to be people of prayer who are ashamed neither of their gifts nor of their heritage as black people.

Conclusion

Such a brief attempt at addressing the spirituality of black people is bound to be limited; however, it may open the door of dialogue. It most certainly has taken place out of the ground of the Second Vatican Council. It is my hope that we will continue the process of *aggiornamento*, continually evaluating and recovering the good things of the past while moving into the future with a renewed vision of Church.

Westerhoff Revisited: Adult Faith Development Suggestions

John R. Zaums

John R. Zaums, Ph.D., is chairperson of the Religious Studies Department, Marywood College, Scranton, Pennsylvania.

1. John H. Westerhoff III, *Will Our Children Have Faith?* (New York: Seabury Press, 1976), 89–103.

2. United States Catholic Conference Department of Education, *1984–1985 Christian Adulthood: A Catechetical Resource* (Washington, D.C.: USCC Office of Publishing and Promotion Services, 1984), 14.

3. John L. Elias, *The Foundations and Practice of Adult Religious Education* (Malabar, Fla.: Robert E. Krieger Publishing Co., 1982), 69.

4. Westerhoff, *Will Our Children*, 93.

One of the most enlightening books in the field of religious education I've had occasion to read since I've been teaching was one published in 1976 by John H. Westerhoff entitled *Will Our Children Have Faith?* Since its appearance, it has, at least at the popular level, influenced thinking in the field of religious education like few other books have.

A section of Westerhoff's work that, after ten years, I still find intriguing is the one that deals with his theory of faith development.[1] For a few moments I'd like to revisit Westerhoff in order, first, to think through some implications of his theory for those of us who work in the field of adult religious education and, second, using some of his insights as a springboard, to make some suggestions for fostering faith development among adults.

In a quite simple but insightful fashion, Westerhoff discusses faith from a developmental perspective. To illustrate his position, he draws upon the analogy of a tree viewed at various stages of development. The tree, at each stage, remains a real tree—the same tree—the only difference being one of degree of maturity. In an analogous way, believers pass through "stages" of faith development on their way toward Christian maturity. For Westerhoff, this faith development manifests itself in various "styles" of faith expression: (1) experienced faith; (2) affiliative faith; (3) searching faith; (4) owned faith. Before briefly describing each style, as well as the implications of each for the field of adult religious education, I want to stress, as does Westerhoff, the fact that real faith is present at each and every step of faith development; the child, as much as the adult, really believes. But, experienced faith does differ from owned faith in terms of maturity, just as a one-year-old sapling differs from a one-hundred-year-old more fully developed tree.

1. Experienced faith. This is the style of faith of the young child. If a five-year-old could find the words to answer the question, "Why do you believe?", one answer might be, "I believe because my parents believe." This is extrinsic faith, a faith outside oneself, a faith in the faith of others. John Elias comments that the child "generally tags along in the [faith] journey of others: parents, sisters and brothers, teachers, and church leaders."[2] At this period of faith development, the witness of parents is of most importance to the child. Commenting on Erik Erikson's thinking, Elias states, "It is in infancy that the journey of faith begins. . . . Religious faith . . . builds upon the trust developed in infants through the loving care of parents."[3] Therefore, comments Westerhoff, what parents must do, if faith is to begin to develop, is to "provide an environment of sharing and interaction. . . . The responsibility of Christian parents is to endeavor to be Christian with their children."[4] As most of us know from personal experience, a teacher may have little, if any, effect upon a child if parents do not witness to their faith. Thus, there is a great need for the adult religious educator to pay close attention to the needs and faith development of parents and to the importance of parent education and parental involvement in the education of their children.

2. Affiliative faith. This style of faith may begin to emerge during the period of adolescence, providing the needs that ground experienced faith have been adequately met. Whether young or old, persons with this style of faith desire to assume a more active part in the life of the faith community. According to Westerhoff:

> All of us need to feel we belong to a self-conscious community. . . . Persons with affiliative faith need to participate in the community's activities—for example, serving at a fellowship supper, singing in the choir, having a part in the Christmas pageant, participating in a service project, belonging to a group in the church where they know everyone's name and they are missed when absent. Of crucial importance is the sense that we are wanted, needed, accepted, and important to the community.[5]

Religious educators need to realize that, for those in the process of developing an affiliative style of faith, "religion of the heart" may be much more critical than "religion of the head." Here, individuals need to be provided with opportunities for experiencing awe, wonder, and mystery, as well as chances to sing, serve, join hands, and celebrate. "How needed and how deeply one feels"—not only "how much one understands"—this must be the focus of our educational activity.

When affiliative faith develops, however, it does not mean that the first style of faith is no longer of importance. Adolescents and adults, as much as young children, still need the witness of others—parents, clergy, teachers—to encourage their growth in faith as they strive to play a more active role in the life of the faith community. To foster such witnessing must be viewed as a major priority for the adult religious educator.

3. Searching faith. This style of faith generally manifests itself during the period of young adulthood which, as I understand the period, begins in the late teens and carries over into the twenties. Since the period of young adulthood is often ignored in discussions of adulthood, I'd like to take some time to describe it and, then, to trace some of its implications for adult religious educators. The need to consider seriously this period was brought home to me quite pointedly in a seminar I taught last year to religious studies majors. The average age of students in the class was about twenty-five. I had assigned a group of articles to read on adult religious education, and among them were two articles on the period of young adulthood. For many students, these proved to be the most popular of all because, finally, as one student commented, someone in the Church had recognized and taken them seriously, the "limbo generation"—that generation of adults out of high school but not yet married.

At a certain point in the young adult's faith life, doubts and questions, often accompanied by a great deal of confusion, begin to appear. Westerhoff believes that this searching style of faith is of critical importance and, in fact, is even necessary if faith, at its more mature level, is to develop. For, as Shirley Kerr comments, "Movement, wrestling, combat and conflict are the crucible out of which [mature] faith is produced."[6]

Many adults, including parents and educators, have mixed feelings about this style of faith. Some are merely uncomfortable in the presence of young adults, while others feel that young adults, who are searching, questioning, and openly doubting, are losing their faith. Westerhoff sharply disagrees with this more traditional, negative approach to questioning and searching. According to him, in order to move from affiliative

5. Ibid., 94.

6. Shirley Kerr, "Morality and Faith from a First World–Third World Perspective," *Religious Education* 80 (Spring 1985): 191.

faith to an understanding of faith that is our own, "we need to doubt and question that faith."[7]

Our task then, as adult educators, is to lead young adults to mature faith, to a point where they can, on their own, make a free, personal and active response to God. In order to do so, we must begin to affirm the value of searching faith and actively create an environment that can help young adults, in their questioning and searching, to experience God's presence, an experience that ultimately grounds owned faith.

But, how successful have adults, including parents, educators, and clergy, been in encouraging the search? How helpful have they been to young adults in their struggles? According to Westerhoff:

> It appears, regretfully, that many adults in the Church never had the benefit of an environment which encouraged searching faith. And so they are often frightened or disturbed by adolescents who are struggling to enlarge their affiliative faith to include searching faith. Some persons are forced out of the Church during this state and, sadly some never return; others remain in searching faith for the rest of their lives. In any case, we must remember that persons with searching faith . . . need to be encouraged to remain within the faith community during their intellectual struggle, experimentation and first endeavors at commitment.[8]

Thus, young adults should be encouraged by the community to work out their questions while remaining within the faith community. While doing so, we must remember that young adults, just as much as children and adolescents, still need to experience the lived witness of others who encourage their growth in faith, as well as to experience a community in which they feel needed, welcomed, helped, and supported.

In other words, if young adults are to own their faith, we, as adult religious educators must help them by providing occasions, creating situations, in which they can, within the context of community, experience God as answer to their searchings. I'd like to present four specific situations in which young adults, with the help and encouragement of educators, can hopefully experience God and grow in faith.

The *educational situation* is the one with which most of us are familiar. When dealing with young adults in this setting, whether that setting be a college religion class, the RCIA, a young singles' discussion group, an engaged encounter, a young marrieds' group, or a baptism preparation class for parents, we ought to assume the presence of questioning, doubting, but open individuals and do everything possible to help them through their doubts and questions about religion, themselves, and their world.

In the educational situation, one of the primary tasks of adult religious educators, in working with young adults, must be to foster the searching process. I believe that in every truly human question there is contained a hint or trace of the divine. It may be that a growing number of young adults are finding it increasingly more difficult to experience God in our secularized world of today, but they may still be able to discover traces of God in the questions they ask of themselves and their world. If traces or hints of the divine are indeed contained in questions that speak to the meaning of human existence, then young adults, in order to become

7. Westerhoff, *Will Our Children,* 96.
8. Ibid., 97.

24

conscious of these hints, must be helped to become aware of, and encouraged to ask, such questions. By so doing, educators may be instrumental in helping them experience, possibly for the first time, the presence of God—an experience of closeness that will hopefully lead them to a life of mature faith.

The *liturgical situation* is one filled with possibilities for religious experience and faith development. On many occasions, students have related to me, both within and outside of class, experiences that they've had while participating in Masses, rites of reconciliation, prayer services, and other liturgical and paraliturgical celebrations—experiences that, in some cases, have radically changed their lives. Thus, in ministering with young adults, we as adult educators must try to take advantage of the infinite possibilities for faith development that liturgy offers.

The *retreat/encounter situation* ought to occupy a central place in any religious education program for young adults. I have consistently found day and weekend experiences for the single, engaged, and married to be most powerful sources for faith development. Such opportunities, wherever and whenever available, ought to be fostered actively.

The fourth situation is one I'll call the *social action situation*. During the searching years, young adults need to experience older adults as well as other young adults who, in their daily lives, give witness to what they believe by their loving concern for others. A church community, aware of the needs of the neighbor both locally and globally and committed to a multileveled program of social action, will do more to attract young adults and help them grow in faith than will all the slick tricks and gimmicks that presently cram religious education textbooks and publishing house catalogs.

Churches ought to be providing, and adult religious educators fostering, service projects and programs centering on issues of peace and justice in which young adults can become involved. Working at soup kitchens or shelters; visiting shut-ins; participating in bike- and hike-a-thons to aid the hungry; contributing to canned food and clothing drives; supporting missions and missionaries; visiting hospitals and homes for the elderly; working with the poor and the oppressed—these and countless other social action situations manifest the Christian commitment of those involved and provide a powerful witness to young adults who, many times, are searching for something to believe in and commit themselves to.

4. Owned faith.   For Westerhoff, owned faith is adult faith, mature faith. When you ask a person at this level of faith development, "Why do you believe?", he or she might respond, "I believe because I've done a lot of living, thinking, and praying and, because of this, I've made my personal decision to believe in God. Now I'm trying to become the best possible Christian I can." Before tracing some implications of this fourth style of faith development for adult religious educators, I'd like to give a very brief description of my understanding of owned faith by presenting four of its major characteristics.

Owned faith is *intrinsic* faith, a faith that has been freely internalized. As understood in the documents of Vatican II and by the American bishops in *Sharing the Light of Faith*, intrinsic faith is a free, personal response on the part of the whole person—head, heart, and hands. People who own their faith are their own persons, willing and able to stand up for their own beliefs.

Owned faith is *active* faith. References to growth in faith in terms of action permeate the Vatican II documents, particularly in the *Pastoral Constitution on the Church in the Modern World*, which states, "This faith needs to prove its fruitfulness by penetrating the believer's entire life, including its worldly dimensions, and by activating him toward justice and love, especially regarding the needy."[9] As stated in *Sharing the Light of Faith*, we who own our faith must seek "to live justly, mercifully, and peacefully as individuals, to act as the leaven of the gospel in family, school, work, social, and civic life, and to work for appropriate social change."[10]

Owned faith is *pilgrim* faith. Faith is the journey, an adventure that must be daily undertaken, experienced, and lived. We are pilgrims when it comes to faith; none of us will ever be "fully" mature. The pattern of our existence is one of ongoing development. We're always on the way, working on, striving for.

Owned faith is *tolerant* faith. As pilgrims, we who own our faith must remain open to different educational, social, and theological positions if our understanding of truth is to develop. We do not have a monopoly on truth, and the truth that we possess is incomplete and always in need of further study. Thus, we should be aware that our partial apprehension of truth, which we faithfully proclaim, must always stand under criticism, remain open to new ideas, and be subject to dialogue so that a richer truth can emerge. Opposing positions discussed in honest dialogue should encourage us not only to rethink and rework but to purify and further develop the truth that we partially apprehend and humbly proclaim.

Westerhoff stresses the fact that owned faith is not something totally divorced from the three styles of faith that preceded it. One of the difficulties in imaging faith development in terms of levels or stages is that a disjointed notion is often created. Many people model their understanding of faith development after an image of a four-staged rocket. When the first stage accomplishes its task, it drops off and the second stage takes over only to run its course and be discarded; the third stage performs its function, drops off and, finally, the fourth stage carrying the payload achieves orbit and flies happily on forever. Now, who ever thinks of the first three discarded stages? How quickly their importance is forgotten! A better model for understanding faith development is Westerhoff's model of the tree—a unifying, not disjointed, image. The one-hundred-year-old tree is the same tree as it was when it was one year old, ten years old and fifty years old. The needs of the one-year-old, the ten-year-old and the fifty-year-old tree are the same needs as those of the one-hundred-year-old tree (water, nutrients, etc.) and must be adequately met at every stage of development if the tree is to continue to grow to maturity. In an analogous way, many of the needs that surface in childhood, adolescence, and young adulthood must continue to be

9. Walter M. Abbott, ed., *The Documents of Vatican II* (New York: America Press, 1966), 219.
10. United States Catholic Conference Department of Education, *Sharing the Light of Faith: National Catechetical Directory for Catholics of the United States* (Washington, D.C.: USCC Office of Publishing and Promotion Services, 1979), 96.

met in the later stages of adulthood, even as new needs surface. Now, specifically, What are some of the needs of adults who have reached, or are in the process of developing, an owned style of faith? What implications do these needs have for the adult religious educator?

First of all, adults need to identify with the faith of a community, just as much as do children. Basic to the philosophy of adult religious education is the need for community among persons. Each adult who is going through the process of growth in faith needs the gifts and the support of others. One of the greatest challenges for the adult religious educator is to help form a loving community among adults while, at the same time, respecting the needs and uniqueness of each adult.

Second, adults need to "feel" their way into faith, just as much as do children and adolescents. It is important not only for an adult to call himself or herself a Catholic but also that he or she "feel" Catholic. For Patricia Barbernitz, feeling Catholic means "to feel at home in church worship and activity, to feel accepted within the community, to feel involved in the direction of the parish."[11] A parish, as a community, must be able to say to each adult, "We want you to be part of us!" There is no substitute for genuine expressions of friendship offered by parishioners to each other and to incoming members. Parish envelopes don't welcome! Events such as welcoming meals and liturgies, receptions, and informal gatherings greatly enhance the spirit of community and the feeling of belonging.[12]

Third, adults need to question their faith. An important step in working out a religious education program for adults is to surface religious questions. According to Michael O'Callaghan, "If an adult has stopped asking questions about her or his religious heritage, then no amount of teaching or preaching will be effective. Adults have to be helped to experience once again the excitement of questioning, of searching for some partial yet highly fruitful understanding of the truths affirmed by religious faith."[13] It is important, however, to realize that a religious education program for adults that stresses such questioning can, at times, create discomfort and confusion. But, people who have followed such a program, says O'Callaghan, "are unanimous in their agreement that the process is tremendously liberating. It helps them enormously to understand their Christian heritage in adult terms. . . ."[14]

Fourth, adults need to experience God's saving presence through liturgy and retreat. Through such experiences, one's owned relationship with God further develops and matures. Thus, the adult religious educator needs to be concerned with the quality of liturgy within the parish and must foster active participation at an adult level. Also the adult religious educator must provide occasions for involvement in the retreat/encounter situation, whether that be through Marriage Encounter, Cursillo, traditional retreats, or days of awareness and renewal.

Fifth, adults need to express their faith through action. Some of the most dramatic learning experiences in my life have come not through books or teachers but through doing. I firmly believe that our most powerful growing experiences are doing experiences, times when we've actively lived out what we profess to believe. Thus, the adult educator

11. Patricia Barbernitz, *RCIA: What It Is, How It Works* (Liguori, Mo.: Liguori Publications, 1983), 28.
12. Ibid.
13. *1984–1985 Christian Adulthood*, 93.
14. Ibid., 95.

needs to encourage adults to act upon their belief in whatever setting they find themselves, whether it be at work, in the community, or within the Church. According to Dolores Leckey, "One's work, wherever it is, at home, in church, in the various institutions of society—these are the places where the people are called to be and to act, and as such these places are, at least potentially, places of communion and places of ministry."[15] Thus, Christian action is much more encompassing than doing only "churchy" things like running parish bingos or annual picnics! The real action is in the workplace!

And finally, adults need to experience a Church, a People, that is both open to and tolerant of diversity. We cannot insist on absolute uniformity and agreement among all Catholics on all issues. If this is our sole criterion for church membership, we might find ourselves with very few members! James Fowler contends that only the mature individual who lives a life reflective of a higher level of faith development is capable of adopting a tolerant position. If Fowler is correct in assuming that a position of tolerance is indicative of a higher stage of faith development, it necessarily follows that, if our parishes are to respond creatively and constructively to diversity, they must increasingly become communities of mature Christians who own their faith.[16] Building such communities of tolerance is the adult educator's challenge.

In summary, I'm convinced that a religious education program for young and older adults that addresses only one or another of the situations or needs I've been describing here is an impoverished one. For example, by limiting a program to only the educational situation in which the intellectual needs of adults are solely addressed, we may be effectively limiting a person's ability to experience God more fully and grow more deeply in faith. Without question, a well-thought-out adult religious education program must encompass formal educational programming, but it must also include more informal opportunities for community involvement, social action, worship, and retreat. All are important; each is necessary. Thus, the National Advisory Committee on Adult Religious Education, in adopting such a broad-based understanding, comments that adult religious education must offer a wide variety of "approaches and methods by which believers are continually encouraged and enabled to move toward deeper levels of faith understanding and commitment."[17]

It is a truism to say that every adult is unique. All of us are on a faith journey, but that journey for each of us is individual. Some of us, in our journeying, may be led to an experience of God and a deepening of faith through involvement in liturgy, others through social action, some through educational programming, and still others through retreat experiences. Thus, the more encompassing we make our program, the more opportunities we provide for adults, for ourselves, to grow in faith!

15. Dolores Leckey, "Themes of the Adult Christian Life," *Origins* 14 (February 21, 1985): 591.

16. James W. Fowler, *Stages of Faith* (New York: Harper & Row, 1981), 186–187.

17. National Advisory Committee on Adult Religious Education, *Serving Life and Faith: Adult Religious Education and the American Catholic Community* (Washington, D.C.: USCC Office of Publishing and Promotion Services, 1986), no. 133.

A Shift in Focus

A shift in understanding adult religious education is taking place.[1] Adult religious education is not an isolated program, but rather, it is a faith-formative process that has a complementary relationship with parish liturgical celebrations and social justice efforts. Adult religious education is one aspect of the overarching process of adult faith formation—a process of being shaped by God and of shaping one's faith response.

The adult catechetical process enables a person to hear the Word of God as it is proclaimed in life experiences, personal relationships, crisis moments, church tradition, Scripture, other religious writings, and religious rituals. This results in becoming aware of one's unique spiritual journey. It empowers one to take responsibility for it and to live a life that embodies the gospel values.

Adult religious educators, then, are not just teachers who inform parishioners about Catholic beliefs or challenge them with the latest theological trends. Rather, they are called to be skilled ministers who understand the dynamics of adult faith development, yet respect the uniqueness of the path each walks with God. In light of the Christian community's faith, they assist people to discover their disjointed lives as a unified story of God's creativity, which can take many possible directions.

The development of the above perspective is a crucial challenge for present adult religious educators. It is the foundational step in making parish adult religious education a holistic process that has continuity, is developmental, and is complementary with other parish faith-enrichment efforts. This article takes initial steps in developing the concept of adult religious education as an integrated parish catechetical process.

Some Perspectives on Adulthood and Faith

Theorists describe adulthood from different angles. It is fruitful to place these viewpoints in creative tension and see how each sheds light on the structure, dynamic, and issues of adulthood. Seasons (Levinson) and passages (Sheehy) speak of movement, tension, and crisis as inherent to adulthood. Developmental tasks (Havinghurst) indicate that there are specific needs indigenous to this life period that must be met. Stages (Erikson) in the adult life cycle speak of the desire for intimacy and the eventual acceptance of one's life as it has been lived.[2]

When this approach is applied to theories regarding faith and moral development, useful insights emerge. Both stages of faith (Fowler) and styles of faith (Westerhoff) indicate that faith is integral to daily life and is ever-changing and expanding.[3] Faith expressions mediate life's meaning. Further, they are influenced by an individual's psychological development, creating a need for them to be continuously transformed.

The notion of faith stages describes faith development from the perspective of an individual progressing through successive phases. Eventually, one becomes a person who makes a faith response out of love and a unity with all people. On the other hand, styles of faith focus on

Fostering Adult Faith: An Integrated Approach

Charles F. Piazza

Charles F. Piazza is consultant for Adult Religious Education, Diocese of Oakland.

1. In this article, adult catechesis and adult religious education will be used synonymously because the latter term is more commonly used nationally.
2. For an in-depth study of adulthood, see Daniel J. Levinson, *The Seasons of a Man's Life* (New York: Knopf, 1978); Gail Sheehy, *Passages: The Predictable Crises of Adult Life* (New York: E. P. Dutton, 1976); Robert J. Havinghurst, *Developmental Tasks and Education* (New York: David McKay Company, Inc., 1973); Erik H. Erikson, *Childhood and Society* (New York: W. W. Norton and Company, 1950).
3. For an in-depth study of faith development, see James W. Fowler, *Stages of Faith* (San Francisco: Harper & Row, 1981); John H. Westerhoff III, *Will Our Children Have Faith?* (New York: Seabury Press, 1976).

the individual's struggle to make a response that comes from the heart, reflects one's own beliefs, and is integrated into one's life style.

Moral development theories are challenging. Recent findings indicate that this process is not divorced from the masculine and feminine aspects of human nature. The task of the individual is to develop a moral behavior that has integrated perspectives from one's masculine rights/obligation-orientation (Kohlberg) as well as one's feminine responsibility/relationship-orientation (Gilligan).[4]

While some of these theories describe common aspects of how faith develops during different periods of life and the particular needs it meets, the specific way faith takes shape in peoples' lives is unique to each individual. Life experiences, culture, language, family, and religious upbringing are among the key factors that give rise to its particular expressions. Even personality has a significant influence on faith.

The Adult Catechetical Process: An Integrated Approach

The theories mentioned above have several significant implications for adult catechesis, or adult religious education. First, adult religious education is a process that enables one to understand and express one's unique relationship with God. Since this relationship is ever-changing, the process is ongoing. Second, because adult religious education provides the means for a person to reflect upon life in light of this relationship, its process empowers one to shape life's meaning and direction. Insights gained are often a source of guidance and hope during crisis moments. Third, the process has personal and communal aspects. Adult religious education programs weave together personal religious experiences and planned events. The structured programs need to be flexible and designed to meet the particular faith and life needs of the participants.

The parish is called to be a community where the Word of God is proclaimed, reflected upon, embodied, and celebrated. While the individual is the only one who can give direction to his or her faith development, the parish community can assist in clarifying and giving expression to one's encounters with God. Crucial to the nature of the adult catechetical process are questioning, informing, discerning, integrating, acting, and celebrating.

Questioning. Life is paradoxical. It consists of birth and death; success and failure; community and solitude; joy and sadness; work and unemployment; love and hatred; dreams and despair; freedom and oppression; forgiveness and hardheartedness. God's creative Word is spoken in the midst of life and addresses the joy as well as the brokenness of daily existence. The catechetical process begins with assisting adults to become aware of and to articulate the life questions and issues that arise daily. This is often painful because it means coming to grips with change and personal limitation.

Informing. Once the risk of facing the question or issue is accepted, the next step is to search for information that will resolve it. Parish communities are called to be supportive of this quest. It is their respon-

4. For an in-depth study of moral development, see Lawrence Kohlberg, *The Philosophy of Moral Development* (San Francisco: Harper & Row, 1981); Carol Gilligan, *In a Different Voice: Psychological Theory and Women's Development* (Cambridge, Mass.: Harvard University Press, 1982).

sibility to provide avenues that enable individuals to explore Scripture, church tradition, modern sciences, history, psychology, sociology, etc., in relation to their concern. The objective of this search is not just to gather information but to gain insight. To encourage a broad perspective, questioning, and discussion, parishes should offer a variety of viewpoints on the topic being dealt with.

Discerning and integrating. Most parish programs stop after the previous phase. However, this is the most crucial and difficult one. It involves sifting through the information and making choices. It means struggling to let go of defenses and confronting personal obstacles to change. Through personal reflection and prayer, new and challenging ideas will shape values, attitudes, and perspectives. Life visions will be expanded, the past let go of, and habits altered. Differences may be bridged and diversity in beliefs and choices accepted. Because of the risk, people open themselves in varying degrees to this part of the catechetical process. The dynamics of this phase make it crucial that the adult religious educator be sensitive, with some basic skills in spiritual direction and pastoral counseling.

Putting into action. This phase involves trying new skills or allowing new perspectives to shape decisions. When this involves justice issues, it is important to provide information on specific activities, organizations, and alternatives.

Celebrating. The catechetical process climaxes in celebrating God's liberating and healing presence in life's joys and struggles. Prayer, though, is an integral dimension in each of the previous four phases. Sometimes, it facilitates the transition from one phase to another or is the source of insight into a question. Other times, it is the means through which one is strengthened by the Spirit or comforted by God.

The catechetical process does not end here but begins again. New questions and issues have surfaced that call for exploration and resolution. This leads to an ever-deepening understanding of God, self, human existence, and creation. Through this process, faith is continually reshaped and expanded.

A Unified Parish Catechetical Process

The catechetical process described above perceives growth as occurring through structured and unstructured, cognitive and affective experiences.[5] It is not as ordered and segmented as it appears. In a given situation, it may be found that some of the phases have taken place during the course of daily events, while others need to be structured programs. At times, several phases may occur simultaneously.

The objective is not to use this process only as a pattern for adult religious education sessions and series, but as the foundational model around which a parish plans its faith-formative events. Parish catechetical, liturgical, and pastoral ministers should strive to plan complementary events. Representatives from these groups should meet to plan collaboratively how to address parishioners' pastoral and spiritual needs, while highlighting certain parish concerns that need special attention. This

5. For a fruitful discussion of a spirituality of education that advocates seeing with both the mind and the heart, see Parker J. Palmer, *To Know As We Are Known: A Spirituality of Education* (San Francisco: Harper & Row, 1983).

would ensure that parish faith, moral, and social issues would be responded to consistently and explored in depth. The result would be a unified and integrated parish process of adult catechesis.

The Role and Task of the Parish Adult Religious Education Coordinator

Adult religious educators minister to a wide range of people—singles and families, young adults and older adults, cradle-Catholics and catechumens, free and oppressed, blue-collar workers and executives, veterans and pacifists, married and divorced, to name just a few. The faith needs of these people are not identical nor are they all at the same place in their faith journey.

In light of this, the parish adult religious education coordinator

- must be aware of the faith needs of the parish, as well as resources, programs, and processes that will facilitate the nourishment of the parishioners;
- is central in assisting the development of a coordinated and integrated adult faith formation process for the parish;
- needs to work collaboratively with other parish ministers and be a consultant to them in the areas of adult faith development and adult catechetics;
- assists parishioners in discerning and locating faith enrichment programs, processes, and activities that are directed toward their particular life and faith needs;
- makes sure that faith enrichment opportunities are followed up and that they reach the depth desired by parishioners.

Hints on Developing an Integrated Parish Program

When developing parish adult religious education programs and processes, do not always initiate a new program. First, locate presently existing opportunities of adult faith formation, structured and unstructured. Identify what issues they deal with and promote them. Meet with those who facilitate these activities and discuss how they can be coordinated with your programs. Some key parish efforts that could be enhanced or further developed by adult religious education programs are Sunday liturgies and celebration of sacraments; parish reconciliation and prayer services; home celebrations for families and singles (e.g., Advent, Lent, family religious education components, etc.); parish social justice efforts; ministry to the divorced; ministry to families; parent education classes in parish sacramental programs; RCIA; prebaptismal catechetical programs; ministry to the sick and elderly; marriage preparation sessions; plans to construct or renovate a parish church.

The next step is to identify faith enrichment and leadership training needs of existing parish organizations. After meeting with the members, suggest practical ways to integrate spiritual and educational opportunities into their present meeting schedule.

Lastly, devise enrichment that fills the gaps in the present opportunities. Issues being dealt with by the parish council that call for personal and parish growth are important topics for programs. If possible, try to develop a committee that would plan parish faith enrichment together, particularly for the Advent and Lenten seasons. When planning, try to provide self-directed enrichment that can be done at home, as well as programs that draw people to the parish center.

Concluding Challenges

This approach to adult religious education poses several challenges. Adult religious educators must be recognized, trained, and utilized as ministers skilled in adult faith formation. Since adult catechesis is integral to many parish ministries, dioceses need to explore further avenues that support and foster the emergence of parish adult religious education leadership. Opportunities for leaders to develop their skills, creativity, and ways of collaborating with other ministers must be available on a continuing basis.

More and more dioceses and universities are developing programs to train adult religious educators and coordinators. These programs need to be formative in nature, developing the participants' spirituality and ministerial style, as well as skills and knowledge. If these programs are to develop adult religious education leadership rooted in an integrated catechetical vision, they need to include offerings in adult faith development, liturgy, adult education, catechetics, spirituality, social justice, and pertinent spiritual direction and pastoral counseling skills. It is important that they model and foster both affective and cognitive learning styles.

Central to achieving this integrated approach to adult religious education is that catechetical, liturgical, and pastoral ministers accept the unique role each has in the adult catechetical process. On the national, diocesan, and parish levels, continued efforts must be made to relinquish territorial perspectives and to find ways to work together. With this, will come not only a consistent adult faith formation process but a collaborative style of ministering.

II. PROGRAM DEVELOPMENT

Have you ever given a party—and no one came? Have you ever worked hard and long on a needs assessment effort and a program design—only to have an unexpectedly low (and disappointing) response?

Research has uncovered many reasons for nonresponse of adults to continuing educational events.[1] However, even the manner in which the program planner goes about the needs assessment process may present a hindrance to participation.

Pitfalls

A common method of parish needs assessment uses a written questionnaire. As I have worked with parish adult catechetical teams in the Archdiocese of Indianapolis, I have often watched the needs assessment process, built upon a written questionnaire, get bogged down over a number of possible pitfalls:

- The questionnaire itself is not "home grown." Rather, it is adapted (worse, lifted) from another source, and the content is foreign to the respondents.
- The questionnaire is distributed in a way that is not actually random (thus, not representative) or in a manner that prohibits a high return rate.
- With a high return rate, the adult catechetical team is swamped by the data and is able to digest it in a meaningful fashion only by hours of hand calculation or with the assistance of a computer.

These pitfalls can and should be avoided.[2] If they are not, the net result will be data that is circumspect at best, unusable at worst.

The needs assessment process below has been designed to avoid these pitfalls. It uses very little paper; asks the potential participants to digest the data; and develops/delivers an educational experience directly through the social networks that exist within the parish.

Assumptions

Before offering the process, a few explanatory remarks about its assumptions are in order.

The parish "as a whole" does not exist! Canonically, yes!; sociologically, no! The parish is a network of clusters of people. These clusters can be identified by various "segmentation variables" that the marketing industry uses.[3] However, most parishes do not have their records organized in such a way as to uncover easily these variables. A more realistic approach is to define a parish by identifying the various groups—formal and informal—within it. A key to effective needs assessment is for the adult education program planner to become aware of the segments within the parish and to avoid the temptation to do a needs assessment effort with the entire parish.

Adult religious education is something new for most Catholic parishioners! A common lament of the programmer/planner is that "the same people always respond." The great majority of parishioners have

A Different Approach to Needs Assessment

Matthew J. Hayes

Matthew J. Hayes is director of Religious Education and coordinator of Adult Catechesis in the Archdiocese of Indianapolis.

1. For an overview, see Huey B. Long, *Adult Learning: Research and Practice* (Cambridge, Mass.: Cambridge University Press, 1983), 84–120; see also, Leon McKenzie, "Nonparticipation in Parish Adult Education: An Empirical Study," *Living Light* XV, no. 3 (1978).

2. Two excellent resources are Leon McKenzie, *Decision Making in Your Parish* (Mystic, Conn.: Twenty-Third Publications, 1980); Leon McKenzie, *The Religious Education of Adults* (Birmingham, Ala.: Religious Education Press, 1982), especially Appendix B.

3. For an overview of market segmentation, see Philip Kotter, *Marketing for Non-Profit Organizations* (Englewood Cliffs, N.J.: Prentice-Hall, 1975), 99–110.

not participated in adult education programs; to do so would be an "innovation." Adult religious education program planners are wise to become aware of the research that has been done on the "diffusion of innovations" through populations. An individual makes a decision to adopt an innovation (e.g., to become involved in an adult religious education program) through his or her "interpersonal network"—people who think and act like him or her, whom he or she respects—who are adopting the innovation (i.e., becoming involved); so, the individual becomes open to adopting it. A key to needs assessment is for the adult education program planner to engage in dialogue with the opinion leaders of the interpersonal networks within the parish in order to activate the strong ties between members of the network to enhance motivation and participation.[4]

"Narrow-cast" (not broadcast) adult education efforts! The parish adult education program planner is wise to target segments of the parish for needs assessment efforts and program delivery. This narrow-casting enables a more manageable approach to data gathering, and (keeping in mind the innovation diffusion process) allows for breaking into segments of the parish that have never responded. Peters and Waterman speak of "chunking" as a strategy for management;[5] the segment of those who have never responded is slowly "chipped away at" by focusing upon specific networks within it. A key to needs assessment is for the adult education program planner to solicit needs/interests from a specific target group and deliver a program back through this group.

The scope of adult religious education is wide open! A needs assessment process is often limited from the start by asking only about explicitly religious needs/interests of potential participants. The adult religious education program planner is wise to help potential participants who are involved in a needs assessment process realize that the "agenda" of adult religious learning may go well beyond religious areas.[6]

A Process for Needs Assessment through Market Segmentation

What, then, is a process of needs assessment that avoids these pitfalls and is based upon the foregoing assumptions?

This is a two-part process for the parish adult education committee, entailing three meetings. The first and third meetings are for the committee, itself. The second meeting, involving representatives of a target group, may only include one or two members of the committee. The second meeting could be done with a number of target groups simultaneously (but separately), facilitated by different members of the committee.

Meeting One: Awareness

A. What are the segments of your parish? Make a list parallel to the following: (1) *formal groups:* parent-teachers' organization; men's group; women's group; singles' group; St. Vincent de Paul Society; Booster Club;

4. For an excellent overview of the diffusion process and the role of the "change agent," see Everette Rogers, *Diffusions of Innovations* (New York: Free Press, 1983).

5. Thomas J. Peters and Robert H. Waterman, Jr., *In Search of Excellence* (New York: Harper & Row, 1984), 125–134.

6. See Leon McKenzie, "Foundations: The Scope, Purposes and Goals of Adult Religious Education" in *1983 Christian Adulthood* (USCC Office of Publishing and Promotion Services, 1983), 17–20.

Diocese of Crookston

eucharistic ministers; lectors; CCD parent group; young marrieds' group; seniors' group; parish council committees; (2) *informal groups:* "old guard"; "newcomers"; neighborhood-based groups; work-based groups; "in-crowd"; "poor"; "wealthy."

B. For each group, can you identify any distinctive patterns that are descriptive of it, such as: age; family status; income level; values/attitudes; involvement level in parish. [**NOTE:** It is not necessary to identify these patterns for each segment identified in A. Rather, do any of these groups stand out in regard to these patterns?]

C. For each group identified, how easy is it to determine: its "membership"? its "leaders"?

D. With which group/groups (according to B and C) does the committee wish to work?

Meeting Two: Dialogue

A. In preparation, have the leaders of the group invite a number of individuals (no more than 10–12) who are representative of the group to an evening of dialogue, lasting about two hours, to discuss adult education in your parish—as it might relate to them.

B. Hold the dialogue evening.[7]

(5 minutes) 1. *Introduction/welcome/posing of a question to the group:* "What do you feel parish members would be interested in learning?"[8]

(5–10 minutes) 2. *Silent generation of responses.* Individual reflection and writing.

(30 minutes) 3. *Round robin listing of responses.* Using newsprint/chalkboard, all responses are listed (each one labeled with a letter) until no more are offered.

7. For an overview of the process suggested, see Doe Hentschel, "There's a Method in the Magic: The Nominal Group Process," *Life-Long Learning* (Washington, D.C.: American Association for Adult and Continuous Education, January 1985).

8. Individuals are asked the question this way—rather than being directly asked what he or she is interested in learning—on the assumption that this less direct question is not as threatening. It assumes that individuals will actually respond from his or her perspective, representing his or her segment.

(40 minutes) 4. *Discussion of responses.* Individuals can speak to his or her response, advocate for it, clarify it; individuals can also question other responses. Discussion is timed, limited, and focused upon each response in a serial fashion.

(5 minutes) 5. *Selection of favored responses.* Each person picks three responses that he or she feels are the best responses to the original question and writes each response on a separate 3″ × 5″ card.

(5 minutes) 6. *Ranking of favored responses.* Each person arranges the cards in order of his or her preference, putting a "3" on the most preferred, a "1" on the least preferred.

(10 minutes) 7. *Tally of results.* While the group takes a short break, the facilitator lists the "scores" of each response, showing how many "3s", "2s", "1s", it has received, as well as the total. When the group reconvenes, the three to five most favored responses can be identified.

(10–15 minutes) 8. *Discussion of results.* The entire group views the results and reacts. Possible combination of responses might be noticed and commented upon.

(10 minutes) 9. *Final data gathering.* Through individual response sheets (see sample), participants are asked to react to a list of processes/methods that could be used to address topical areas that have surfaced; potential time slots for learning. These individual sheets are turned in and, subsequently, tabulated by the facilitator.

Meeting Three: Analysis

A. The committee gathers to review the results of the dialogue evening(s). Prior to this meeting, the newsprint/chalkboard information is transcribed and the reaction sheets are tabulated. The committee tries to answer the following questions:

1. Is it within our scope to address the high interest topical areas?
2. Are any of the high interest topical areas already being addressed by an adult education institution in our area?
3. What resources could be used to address the high interest topical areas within our scope?
4. What processes/methods and time-frames seem reasonable?
5. What further information do these topical areas tell us about this target group?

B. The committee *targets* the identified group for promotion about the program. The leaders and participants in the dialogue evening can be asked to distribute flyers and information to members of their groups. In addition, the regular means of promotion (i.e., bulletins, pulpit) can be used in the parish at large.

SAMPLE RESPONSE SHEET

PREFERENCES REGARDING TIME, FORMATS, LENGTH, LOCATION

1. Check your view of the three most convenient times for parishioners to attend programs.

   AM = Morning   PM = Afternoon   EV = Evening

Monday	___AM ___PM ___EV	Friday	___AM ___PM ___EV
Tuesday	___AM ___PM ___EV	Saturday	___AM ___PM ___EV
Wednesday	___AM ___PM ___EV	Sunday	___AM ___PM ___EV
Thursday	___AM ___PM ___EV		

2. Which format(s) do you feel parishioners most prefer? (Please check)

   ____ Lecture Format with opportunity for questions
   ____ Lecture Format with opportunity for group interaction/discussion
   ____ Small-Group Discussion Format with a facilitator
   ____ Small-Group Discussion Format with a study guide
   ____ Other: Describe_____

3. What do you feel is the preferred session length for our parishioners? (check one)

   ____ One Hour
   ____ Two Hours (with break)
   ____ Three Hours (with break)

4. Some programs need more than one session. What do you feel is the *maximum* number of sessions a parishioner would be willing to attend, assuming she/he is interested in the topic? (check one)

____ One-session program only	____ Four-session program
____ Two-session program	____ Five-session program
____ Three-session program	____ Six-session program

5. In what locations do you feel parishioners prefer to attend programs? (check one)

   ____ On parish premises
   ____ In a home in the neighborhood

[**Note to committee:** In formulating these questions, do not list times or places that you are not willing to employ (e.g., if no Sunday programming is desired, do not list it as an option).]

Who is Responsible for Adult Religious Education?

James DeBoy

How would you answer the question: "Who is responsible for adult religious education?" Obviously, those who plan and implement programs are partly responsible. Each individual is also significantly responsible for determining what and how one learns as a self-directing adult. And, it is also true that a person is influenced by a variety of factors in making decisions—people, events, circumstances. Thus, in my experience, three particular groups are responsible for enabling a person's religious growth: the family, the parish community, and those involved as planners and catechists in systematic religious education programs for adults.

The influence of these three groups has been clearly identified in the religious education of children and youth. The bishops of the United States state in *Sharing the Light of Faith: National Catechetical Directory for Catholics of the United States* (NCD):

> A correct understanding of experiential learning includes recognition that the entire faith community is an important part of the experience of children and youth: parents, catechists, and community all have roles in the catechesis of the young (NCD, 181, Section 11).

Granted, this may be true for the religious growth of children and youth, but does it really apply to *adults*? Haven't adults developed their own identity, shaped by their family of origin, but which is now no longer dependent on it? How does the parish community influence adults who now make decisions for themselves? Clearly, program planners and catechists can be an influence, once the adult decides to participate; but, adults have to make that decision first. While it is true that adults have a greater possibility of acting as a result of their own decisions, I am convinced that the three groups mentioned have a significant impact on their willingness and capacity to participate in adult religious education. Let's explore the question further.

Family–Primary Relational Group(s)

With adults, the family of origin may or may not continue to influence their religious growth. Although someone may have moved a great distance from and have little contact with the family, its influence may continue.

The family helped shape the adult's attitude toward learning. For example, does the adult learner actively address questions and seek new information, or does he or she merely adhere to what authority figures say? In either case, one's learning style has been significantly influenced by the family. Has a person developed a love of reading, listening, discussing, interacting as one learns?

If the family's influence is such that it enhances a person's religious development, it can be built upon. If, however, the influence hinders religious development (for example, by placing obstacles to see new and richer insights), it may need to be confronted, challenged and, possibly, rejected.

The reader has probably heard the statement, "I don't know why

James DeBoy is director of the Division of Religious Education in the Archdiocese of Baltimore.

we have all these new changes in the Church. If it was good enough for my parents, it's good enough for me." Such an attitude holds little promise for an adult exploration of the relationship between faith and life.

While the influence of the family of origin may continue either positively or negatively for most adults, other persons and groups will have a greater impact on an adult's attitude toward and participation in adult religious education. These include a person's spouse, close friends, neighbors, associates at work, recreational and leisure groups, and clubs. The influence of media (video, radio, and print media) also impacts how an adult may respond.

Studies have indicated that a person's spouse has a significant influence on participation in a religious group. If one's spouse is actively involved, one is more likely to be involved. This influence can also be a factor in participation in adult religious education.

Attitudes and actions of adults can be influenced by those who are close to them. Many things are discussed during car pools, coffee klatches, bowling groups, lunch groups, dinners, gun clubs, social events, softball games, senior citizen meetings, and other activities. The ability of certain groups to motivate people to write to legislators, contact talk shows, participate in demonstrations and other actions to promote their particular cause is a clear indication of how much adults can be influenced by others. The implications for adult religious education will be explored later.

Parish Community

The influence of the parish community in the continuing religious growth of adults is receiving more attention. Parishes, like families, don't have a choice about whether they will teach the faith. Because they are constantly teaching by their attitudes, actions, values, hospitality (or lack of it), their only choice is whether to teach well or poorly.

The influence of the parish community on a person's desire to participate in continuing learning about faith can be both subtle and pervasive. An important influence is the "tone" of the life of the parish. This is expressed in the way people are welcomed into the parish; the way telephones or parish office doors are answered; the way inquiries are responded to; and the way people are invited to be involved in the life and activity of the parish. Some parishes express a tone of enthusiasm and vibrancy in the way liturgy is celebrated; important issues are addressed; justice and peace activities are carried out; and decisions are made. Other parishes display a very languid or lackadaisical approach to these items—if they address them at all.

The way the parish celebrates liturgy is especially influential in motivating adults to continue to grow in the understanding and living of their faith. The ushers can be warm ministers of hospitality and greet people enthusiastically as they arrive for liturgy, or they can be mere organizers of movement and have little or no interaction with those who come to worship.

A homily can be an opportunity to raise issues for consideration by adults; bring to bear the principles drawn from the Scriptures and the teachings of the Church; suggest possible alternative ways of addressing the issues; and call forth adults to determine for themselves what actions they will take. Or, the homily can be an experience where adults are told what to do in a patronizing tone. Many times, when adults perceive themselves to be treated as children, they will reject the authority that has told them what to do—even when the directive may be a very authentic response to an issue. The problem is often more in the tone and approach of the homilist than in the action that is being offered for consideration.

The experience of liturgy needs to reflect the makeup of the community. Are both men and women involved as lectors, cantors, ushers, eucharistic ministers, and in other ministries? In parishes with a mixed diversity of ethnic and cultural backgrounds, these ethnic and cultural experiences are celebrated in an integral way in the liturgy. In this way, the parish experience of prayer and worship calls forth the richness and gifts of all members of the community for the good of all. When a parish has only one style of celebrating and there is little variety in the liturgical experience, the message is very clearly given that there is only "one way" to do things in this parish. Such an attitude has a very serious impact on adults in the way they participate in the life of the parish, particularly in efforts to help them deepen their understanding and living of the faith.

Parish life is also influential in the way adults are involved in the decision-making processes. Meaningfully involving parish councils and committees and consulting the parish community at-large on important issues are factors in helping adults become more involved in the life of the parish.

Motivation is also enhanced by an active outreach in areas of social justice, in which members of the parish are invited to respond to the needs of the poor, the oppressed, the homeless, and the victims of prejudice.

The tone and life of the parish are significantly guided by the attitudes and personalities of the parish leaders, particularly the pastor. Because they are so visible, the parish clergy have very important influence, and the other parish leaders such as permanent deacons, pastoral associates, catechetical leaders, and others all influence adults by the way they relate to people and respond to the needs of the community. The bishops acknowledge this influence of the parish:

> The total learning environment of the parish is also an important factor in motivating adults. This includes the quality of the liturgies, the extent of shared decision making, the priorities in the parish budget, the degree of commitment to social justice, the quality of the other catechetical programs. Programs for adults should confront people's real questions and problems honestly and openly (NCD, 189).

Through these and in many additional ways, the parish community is constantly catechizing parishioners about their importance, or lack of it, in the life of the parish and in the Church's mission to transform society through proclaiming and bringing about the reign of God.

Systematic Adult Religious Education

The third important group that influences the continued learning of adults is those people who serve as planners, coordinators, and catechists in systematic efforts to provide adult religious education. Much has been said about the importance of designing such programs in accord with good principles of adult learning. It is also important to have a variety of learning programs, topics, and learning activities to respond to the varying learning preferences, interests, and needs of adults in the parish. In addition to these factors, programs for adult religious education need to be held in a variety of settings (e.g., rooms designed for adults in the parish hall, in homes or other meeting places in the parish or in nearby agencies or institutions). These learning environments need to be attractive, comfortable, and clearly meant for adults.

Readers of this and previous volumes of *Christian Adulthood* are already aware of the importance of such factors in promoting continued learning by adults. The bishops have stated:

> The best inducement to participate is an excellent program. People are drawn by the testimony of satisfied participants, as well as by personal invitations from friends and Church leaders (NCD, 189).

In addition to these factors, a critical element is the way program leaders and catechists deal with adults. Do these people invite adults to reflect on their own experiences and discuss them with one another before a presentation is made or a particular action is suggested? Or, do the leaders tell adults what they think should be done and only then invite questions or reactions? In my experience, the attitude and tone of the presenter have proven to be critical factors in inviting a response from learners. Dealing with questions respectfully and sensitively—even when the questioner's point of view is significantly different from that of the presenter—is extremely helpful in establishing relationships of trust and respect. In such an atmosphere, difficult and delicate issues can be addressed with sensitivity and concern, even in the midst of a wide variety of opinions and attitudes. Those who serve as planners, coordinators, and catechists in programs for adult catechesis need to be very concerned about the style with which they relate to adult participants.

Implications for Adult Religious Education

If the analysis of these three groups is accurate, there is a need to explore the implications for adult religious education. The first implication is that adult catechesis does not begin when a person reaches the age of eighteen or twenty-one. The foundations of adult catechesis are actually being laid in the later years of a person's family life and the early years of one's education. The attitude one has toward learning (whether it is open and inquiring or closed and hesitant) is significantly shaped by one's family and early teachers. Therefore, those responsible for planning and implementing programs for adult religious education need to be aware of and concerned about the quality of other religious education programs for children and youth in the parish. Second, those involved in adult religious education need to be aware of the civic, social, and leisure groups in which adults in the parish tend to participate. In so doing, they can note their possible influence, taking advantage of the positive aspects and working to diminish any negative aspects. Adult religious educators might also consider the possibility of establishing neighborhood groups throughout the parish that would provide the opportunity for adults to meet people who share the same neighborhood and parish experiences. In this way, it might be possible to provide adults with new group experiences that can reinforce the life that the parish is trying to promote. Program efforts for a comprehensive approach to parish renewal, such as RENEW, have tried to develop small-group communities in the parish and have met with some success.

Those involved in adult religious education also need to be aware of the tone and life of the parish community at-large. This tone and life can positively influence continued learning by adults in a parish, or it can be an obstacle to it. The parish community is always teaching by its actions, attitudes, and values and by the way it deals with disagreements and issues. The first step is to be aware of the life of the parish and then, if need be, to initiate efforts to enhance or redirect it. The attitudes and relational styles of other parish leaders are significant aspects of the tone and life of the parish. It might not be possible to change people, but it is important to be aware of what is happening.

The implications are clear for the preparation of those who serve as catechists for adults. Program leaders need to relate well with adults and deal with sensitive and delicate issues maturely. Not everyone is equally skilled, so care should be taken in choosing leaders and presenters in programs for adults. At the same time, with the advances of technology and the variety of media that are now available, an "expert" could be brought in via videotape or film, and a parish person could be trained to facilitate the discussion, using the media to stimulate interaction among the learners.

One of the most important implications is that people who deal with adults need to be able to engage them in the process of critical thinking and dialogue. It is important that the Church's teaching be brought into the discussion, but I have found that adults are much more willing to listen to and carefully consider the teachings of the Church when their own experiences and concerns have been elicited and listened to.

Adults are self-directing; they will decide what they want to do. Very often, the best that adult religious educators can do is to offer possible alternatives for their consideration. Telling adults that "this is what you must do" often produces the opposite result. The freedom of adults to decide for themselves is an essential principle that should guide all interaction with them. The American bishops have stated:

> The act of faith is a free response to God's grace; and maximum human freedom only comes with a self-possession and responsibility of adulthood. This is one of the principal reasons for regarding adult catechesis as the chief form of catechesis (NCD, 188).

When the three groups—family–primary relational group, parish community, and those involved as planners or leaders in adult religious educational programs—all work together, the possibility of influencing and motivating adults to continue their religious learning is extremely powerful. When these three groups offer divergent or conflicting perspectives, it becomes much more difficult for adults to continue their learning. No situation will be perfect, but if planners are aware of the influence of these groups, their planning can be more realistic. It may even be possible to bring about changes so that these groups can work more closely and powerfully together to enable adults to grow in faith and to live it each day.

Planning Creative Adult Religious Education Leadership Programs

Charles F. Piazza and M. Sheila Collins

More and more dioceses are discovering that it is necessary to start programs that develop parish leaders' understanding and skills in adult religious education. After planning begins for such programs, initial enthusiasm often wanes because of the numerous questions and issues that arise. These questions range from concerns about the program's structure to training methodology to whom the program will serve.

This article outlines simple planning steps and offers insights into key questions that arise during the planning period. The concepts presented here are the result of a process that the Oakland diocese is presently engaged in for developing adult religious education leadership.

Step I

Consider: What Type of Program Is Needed by Parish Adult Religious Education Leaders? What Needs Will It Meet?

The process begins by consulting parish leaders regarding their specific adult religious education leadership needs. Adult catechesis is an integral part of many parish ministries. Also, effective adult religious education does not occur in isolation from other opportunities that enrich faith. Because of this, among those who need to be consulted are RCIA directors, adult religious educators, those who train liturgical ministers, master catechists, those who conduct prebaptismal and marriage preparation sessions, and directors of religious education.

The consultation centers on how the diocese can assist these leaders in assuming their responsibility of providing effective and sound adult faith enrichment. This discussion surfaces the adult faith development topics to be explored, adult religious education principles and techniques to be learned, and adult catechetical skills to be developed. The time commitment leaders are able to make and their desire for an extensive program or series of sessions will be indicated during the consultation.

Step II

Determine: What Are the Focus and Objectives of the Program?

A period of sifting through and prioritizing the information received follows the consultation process. In light of the specific information gathered and basic adult faith formation principles, the focus and objectives of the program are reached.

When developing the program's focus, keep in mind that adult religious education does not occur in isolation. Structured adult religious education programs and processes are only one key aspect of adult faith formation, a process of being shaped by God's activity and of shaping one's faith response. Integrated adult faith formation and adult religious education involve a conscious, collaborative effort among parish catechetical, liturgical, and pastoral ministers.

Besides the trainees' acquisition of a basic understanding of how

Charles F. Piazza and M. Sheila Collins are, respectively, consultants for Adult Religious Education and Family Centered Catechesis in the Diocese of Oakland.

adults grow in faith and skills in adult faith formation, other important activities for them are

- being introduced to a variety of styles of spirituality and learning how to apply the underlying theories and techniques in their ministry;
- developing an understanding of their ministry and a process of ministering that can be applied in their pastoral situation;
- learning effective ways to use Scripture in their own faith journey and how to enable others to do the same;
- becoming aware of their personal creativity and fostering its growth;
- developing skills in theological reflection and self-directed learning.

Step III

Develop: What Are the Program's Structure and Process?

The basic structure of the program needs to have three components: (1) an overview of adult faith formation and/or adult religious education; (2) specialized training in specific ministries in relation to adult faith formation; and (3) a period of ministerial internship. The program's process needs to be formative in nature and include didactic learning, skills development, and personal faith enrichment. The above can take shape in learning sessions, integrative seminars, self-directed learning packets, prayer experiences, spiritual direction, and supervised internship experiences. It is also valuable to consider providing participants with a mentor experience in their particular ministry.

In order to reflect the program's values of a holistic process, it is ideally designed and implemented by a team representing a variety of ministerial interests and experiences. (The planning steps outlined here were, in fact, developed by a team.) The team models and seeks to develop a process reflecting mutuality and collaboration in ministry. The planning team for the process may become the coordinating team for the program. This maintains continuity between the planning and implementation stages and ensures the representation of the varied ministerial disciplines in a visible and active way. In forming the team, experience and expertise must be present in a variety of areas: catechetics, spirituality, psychology, liturgy, and pastoral care. An awareness of physical development, sociological realities, and justice issues must also be evident.

We suggest that each member of the team be involved in the planning and implementation of the program; the team as a whole struggles to develop ideas, concepts, and processes. The aim of the team's efforts cannot be simply to present a prepackaged program. The process developed for the participants must uniquely reflect the needs identified in Step I.

Through the program, the team can provide and model a flexible process for the participants that would allow them to develop an adult education leadership program for the people with whom they work.

The goals of the program must be evident in the qualities that characterize it. Some characteristics to be considered are the following:

Holistic. Will the program address the person as an integrated whole (spiritually, psychologically, physically)?

Creative. Will the program enable the participants to value and utilize their own creativity?

Integrative. Will the program allow the participants to make the skills and insights that they experienced part of their own ministerial style?

Experiential. Will the program encourage the participants to learn by doing?

Self-Directive. Will the program see both presenters and participants as learners and teachers?

Individualized. Will the program meet the specific ministerial needs of each participant?

Formational and informational. Will the program provide for both affective and cognitive learning?

Aesthetic. Will the setting for the program be conducive to both left- and right-brained teaching methods?

Justice-oriented. Will the program enable each participant to embody a ministerial style that is rooted in gospel values?

It is important that the program's designers be aware of other key characteristics that may surface as the program is being planned and developed.

A Family Sensitivity in Adult Religious Education

Thomas F. Lynch

In this article, I wish to address the interplay between the individual, the family, and intentional learning experiences. In particular, I will focus on learning experiences that foster change in a person's attitudes, behaviors, or values and their possible implication for the family.

I am sure that we can all recall stories of persons who attended workshops, courses, and renewal programs that had a profound effect on their lives. From these experiences, they had the courage to change and to relate differently to others. A story may help illustrate this point.

I remember a woman who, while attending a charismatic prayer meeting, was "baptized in the Spirit." This experience deeply affected her. As a result, she began to relate differently to her family. She tried to get the other family members to share in her experience and to pray with her. In response, they became uncomfortable. First, they humored her; then, they tried to change her back to the way she used to be. Over a period of time, tension and alienation grew between them.

Reflection questions: Do you know of similar stories? How would you describe them? What could have been done to help the participants and their families deal more constructively with the changes that were initiated by the learning process?

Clearly, a family perspective in our educational programs is an important consideration in helping families deal with change. There are several points that I wish to develop that will help you to incorporate such a perspective into your programs. First, I will list them and then explain each in turn.

1. An individual needs to live in a series of relationships in order to continue to grow as a person. One of the most important of these is family.

2. The family establishes its own identity and way of operating. Each member plays various roles that help the family function and maintain its identity. Out of these roles, family members learn patterns of relating. These are frequently carried over to other relationships and groups.

3. When a family member changes his or her way of relating, the change will impact on other family members. It will challenge them to change how they relate to that person. This challenge often induces stress and tension within the family.

4. Families respond differently to changed members. How a family responds depends upon whether it needs to maintain the status quo or whether it senses a need to initiate change in order to grow.

5. There is a need for church ministries to use processes that help both individuals and families to become sensitive to the various dynamics at work within the family.

Before commenting on each of the above points, I would like to describe my understanding of *family.* "A family is two or more persons related by blood, marriage or adoption, founded and given life by love."[1] Family also includes one's family of origin (extended and nuclear), one's ancestors, and various kinship networks.

Now to explain each point.

1. The human person is relational by nature. For an individual to

Thomas F. Lynch is a priest of the Diocese of Bridgeport and director, Office for Marriage and Family Life, National Conference of Catholic Bishops.

1. Commission on Marriage and Family Life, United States Catholic Conference, *A Family Perspective on Church and Society,* draft statement (Washington, D.C.: USCC Department of Education, 1986), 12.

grow, he or she needs relationships that will provide a sense of belonging, self-esteem, and a conviction of being loved. Only within these relationships can a person realize his or her potential. Individuals seek to meet their basic needs in relational communities, which are either friendship or family-based. I will focus on the latter.

It is within the family that one first experiences relationships. These relationships, in turn, color how one relates to life, to others, and to God. The family's influence will also shape a person's identity and values.

From research, it is becoming clearer that families have tremendous influence on their members throughout life. One is never free from family influence, even if physically removed from it. The power of this influence is evident in the individual's constant effort either to copy or redo initial familial experiences in later relationships.

Reflection questions: How did your family originally influence you? How is it still influencing you?

2. Each family "assigns" roles to its members in order to function. These roles help family members learn appropriate ways of relating so that the family can maintain its identity.

In assigning these roles, the family addresses the issues of cohesion and adaptability. Family cohesion helps the members deal with the difficult issue of balancing mutual support and independence relative to other family members. Cohesion also pertains to how opened or closed the family, as a whole, will be with the other communities. Family adaptability helps the members address the issues of how flexible or stable its structure must be so that they will be able to meet their own needs and the needs of the family.[2]

As the family works out the issues of cohesion and adaptability and assigns different roles, it begins to have a unique sense of its own identity. It becomes the "Lynch" family or the "Smith" family, with its unique characteristics.

Family cohesion is worked out concretely in the areas of support, closeness, decision making, commonality, and family unity.[3] For example, regarding commonality, a family will fall somewhere on the continuum between doing very little to doing everything together. It seeks to live in a creative balance between being too connected (enmeshed) or too separated (disengaged). *Enmeshed* means that individuals are not easily permitted their own identity outside of the family. *Disengaged* means that family members have little sense or appreciation for family unity. They may share the same household, but they are essentially isolated from each other. As a family determines how separated or connected its members will be, it assigns appropriate roles to each.

Reflection questions: How did your family work out the issues of cohesion? What roles were assigned to you and to other members of the family? How have these roles changed through the different stages of the family life cycle?

The issue of adaptability is worked out concretely in the areas of leadership, discipline, negotiations, organization, and values.[4] An ex-

2. See Kathleen Galvin and Bernard Brommel, *Family Communication: Cohesion and Change* (Glenview, Ill.: Scott, Foresman and Company, 1986).

3. See Patrick Carnes, *Understanding Us* (Minneapolis, Minn.: Interpersonal Communication Programs, Inc., 1981).

4. Ibid.

ample is how a family deals with setting limits and carrying out consequences. In this regard, a family will fall somewhere on the continuum between strict and permissive. The family will struggle to live in a creative balance between being flexible and stable without pushing itself to the extreme positions of rigidity or chaos.

Reflection questions: How did your family address the issue of adaptability? Did the family respond differently at various stages in its life cycle?

As the family seeks its identity, and as its members assume their respective roles, these experiences begin to shape their ways of relating, which are manifested in behaviors, attitudes, and values. Family members will also seek to duplicate their familial structure within other structures that they enter.

3. A family member enters a new group with set ways of relating. If these ways cause conflict within the group, the group will challenge the person to change. Should change occur, it could have consequences for relational patterns within the family.

Reflection questions: Can you recall a time when your way of relating was altered by a group? Did this new way of relating have an effect on your family relations?

Many programs in the Church seek to call people to conversion by challenging them either to deepen or to change their ways of relating. Some examples are the following:

a) intensive weekend experiences and ongoing ministerial programs for youth, young adults, singles, engaged couples, marrieds, those who are separated or divorced, etc., that seek to change or deepen attitudes, values, behaviors, and life skills;
b) formational programs (e.g., religious education, school, campus ministry, adult education) that seek to root one's faith in the ongoing tradition and service of the Church, thereby challenging present ways of relating.

For a more detailed listing of programs, please consult the *Family Perspective* paper of the Marriage and Family Commission, United States Catholic Conference.[5]

Reflection question: What have you ever experienced in a church program that influenced you to change your way of relating to other persons?

It is important for church leadership to be sensitive to how they may change a person's way of relating to self, to others, and to God. If, through our programs, someone begins to develop a new way of relating and attempts to incorporate this change into his or her life, there would be an impact on the rest of the family. It may affect the role that person plays within the family and cause the family to relate differently to him or her.

If the family wishes to relate differently to the changed person, the

5. Commission on Marriage and Family Life, *A Family Perspective.*

other family members either have to change themselves or live with the tension and stress that result from the changed situation. In other words, if one family member changes, the whole family will be challenged to change.

4. Although change in a family may seem natural, it can cause serious stress. In facing a changed member, the family either seeks to maintain its present way of relating (status quo) or searches for a new way.

To maintain the status quo and minimize change, the family will address the changed person in the following ways:

a) by conscious or unconscious pressure to resume former roles, attitudes, values, or behaviors;
b) by exclusion or expulsion;
c) by resigning itself to live with both the changed individual and the resulting tensions.

Reflection questions: Do you remember a time when your family resisted change? What were the circumstances?

When the family possesses a more change-promoting attitude, its members will begin the process of changing themselves in relation to the changed person and to each other. In this position, the family has a sense that, for it to continue to exist in a life-giving manner, it must change.

However, change within other family members is often difficult because they may have to deal with issues that they have not yet faced. An example would be a family that must face up to greater self-disclosure in response to a member that has experienced its benefits.

Because change is often slow and painful, it may cause the family to switch back to former ways of interacting, thereby resisting the adjustments necessary for growth.

Reflection question: Recall a time when your family was faced with change. How was each member affected?

5. Ministerial and educational programs within the Church need to become sensitive to family relationships. These relationships greatly influence the ability of a person to change. The family can sabotage our best efforts if it seeks to maintain its status quo in ways of relating and of assigning roles. By building into our programs a process that will help both the individual and the family deal with change, we can minister more effectively and responsibly.

It is, therefore, important to incorporate into our programs materials and processes that help participants deal with issues of cohesion and adaptability within their respective families. In particular, we need to help them reflect on how their families have already worked out these issues. We need to help them see and understand the roles that they and other members play within the family. We also need to help them discern whether their families are open or closed to change and what may be the implications if they change. We can also help them to identify other family members who would support their change and who would help the family change its ways of relating and of assigning roles. Finally, we can help participants dream of how they would like their families to be relating in the future. In so doing, they can reflect on how realistic their dreams are and on what skills and knowledge are needed by the family in order to realize them.

There may also be a need to support both the individual and the family with personal and financial resources until the desired change has been securely adopted.

You may find the reflection questions used in this article helpful in incorporating family sensitivity into your programs. If, realistically, all you can do is to be sensitive to the interaction among the family members, you still have made great strides in developing a family perspective in your programs.

Bringing a family perspective into our educational programs is certainly something with which few of us are accustomed. Yet, without doing so, we run the risk of having our otherwise good efforts go for naught. It is hoped that, having had the opportunity to reflect on our own family backgrounds, we are more sensitized to the far-reaching implications of the family's impact on those of its members who are the subjects of our ministry.

III. LEADERSHIP AND PROFESSIONAL DEVELOPMENT

At thirty-six, Rita made a difficult decision. She left the Catholic Church and joined the Assembly of God. "It's not that there's anything wrong with the Catholic Church," she admitted, "it's just not enough!"

Is Rita's decision justified? Are others making similar choices? Mounting evidence supports the fact that a number of Catholics are becoming affiliated with other Christian denominations, often fundamentalist. Should we be concerned? Does this represent a significant trend? There is a plethora of reasons for such disaffiliation. A leader in the Assembly of God in my area states quite candidly that 75% of his people are former Catholics. He offers the following reasons why Catholics are leaving us and joining him: we do not listen to peoples' needs, and we fail to offer hospitality. Whatever the cause, there is a value at issue here that strikes at the heart of the adult Catholic faith.

World View

As philosophical and sociological world views have changed so have individual adult world views. People interpret their lives, and correspondingly their religious faith, from a perspective quite different than in previous eras. How so? Many would describe the phenomenon as a shift from assent to authority for meaning to one's individual search for meaning. Adults who formerly would have lived with less-than-meaningful religious practices and less-than-adult challenges in the Church are confronting these issues in a definitive way. They're voting with their feet. They are leaving us!

There's a real sociological shift here. Once a Catholic, always a Catholic formerly described membership. Today, Catholics are choosing other alternatives. Even the new Code of Canon Law recognizes this. Those who formally join another Church are no longer to be considered Catholic as implied in canon 1086.[1]

Theology and Therapy

Catholicism is a theologically centered community rooted in doctrine, tradition, Scripture, and discipline. There's security in being a Catholic. It is a religion with its memory intact. We know from whence we've come, where we are, and where we will be. This implies, of course, that one has, to some degree, internalized the external Catholic symbol system. However (and this is not meant to demean the invaluable service of many in works of Christian charity), we have not been known as a community of hospitality. Inasmuch as we have been definitively theological, we have not been decidedly therapeutic!

We might say we have emphasized external appropriation of the faith to the diminution of internal appropriation. Consider Rita's situation. Although baptized and raised a Catholic, she found the doctrinal and sacramental life of the Church she experienced insufficient for her needs. Her internalization of the faith was hampered from becoming her meaning system in the Catholic sense. Rita had problems. Nevertheless, she found no therapy in the institutional Church to meet her emotional/

Ministry to Adults in a Changing World

Gregory Michael Smith

Gregory Michael Smith, Ed.D., is a priest and chancellor and secretary of Education for the Diocese of Bridgeport.

1. James A. Cordien, Thomas J. Green, and Donald E. Heintschel, *The Code of Canon Law, A Text and Commentary* (New York: Paulist Press, 1985), 768.

spiritual needs. Apparently, she did find this answer with the Assembly of God.

Adult Transition

Adults are in transition. This is a well-established fact from both sociological and psychological research. Adults also have religious needs that transcend the heretofore clear lines that once differentiated theology and therapy. Had Rita found sympathetic Catholics to affirm her transition, offering hospitality and agreeing to walk with her in her time of need, she might possibly be with us today. Anthropology and spirituality confirm this human dimension.

We have not been listening to people's spiritual cries for help. We have been too busy protecting truth. If, as some scientists are saying today, life is a tandem of cognitive and affective domains, the Church has steadfastly failed in the latter. We have acted as if intellectual powers sufficed for living faithfully. Had we come to terms with the Gospel's sense of compassion, much of our theological strengths might also have been therapeutically sound.

The State of Life

The world of the post-modern adult is not the world of our forebearers. It differs specifically in the following ways.

1. Elongated life span. With a life span extending to eighty years for many, both the possibility and the opportunity for wider life experiences exist. The adult of today knows that life will be filled with stretched seasons of change, redirection, and maturity. What once had to fit into forty years can be postponed for later development.

As people survive longer, their material, physical, emotional, and spiritual needs are affected. The spiritual life also has a wider margin. We can appreciate this as a blessing in the sense of having more time for gathering depth in life or as a delaying tactic for spiritual decisions. Whichever, the longer time we have the more we have to enjoy possibilities previously unattainable. And so, aging involves the struggles with transitions previously unlivable. This has direct and specific bearing upon adult ministry.

2. Unlimited life opportunities. As a consequence of expanded lifetimes, along with affluence, the post-modern adult in our first world context enjoys virtually limitless possibilities for living life more fully. No longer citizens of a narrow village-oriented world, we are seekers in a galactic venture. Quite possibly, some of us will be space voyagers. For the rest, spinoffs and breakthroughs in science and technology will afford us possibilities for living, unheard of in all of previously recorded history. Such possibilities have already changed us. They will also threaten us and tempt us with experiences once culturally unacceptable. In a world of sudden change, replete with both moral and immoral opportunities, our spiritual potential will be challenged in remarkably exciting and ominous ways.

Diocese of Owensboro

3. Changing symbols. Those intangible meaning systems that previously described life are changing. And, since these meaning systems are life's sustaining values, their change will challenge life's principles.[2] Symbols bring into life's meaning system a conscious appreciation of ultimate values worth struggling for. Permanency, for example, was once an ultimate adult value. Practically speaking, it no longer is. Modern life is built upon moveable feasts, alternating customs, and marketable fashions.

As traditional markers of healing and compassion become invisible in traditional institutions like the Church, adults are turning to new markers of hospitality—wherever they are found! We must remind ourselves that people once set free from traditional moorings (as in the sociological phenomena of post-Vatican II and *Humanae Vitae*) find their own philosophical center and collective rituals. Here, adults come of age despite us.

As we begin to appreciate life through the eyes of new symbols, and as once dearly held values waver and fade, our lives inalterably change. This affects how we view religious truth and how spiritual needs are resolved. Consequences of these changes are apparent in our marriages, family life, identification with Church, and commitments.

4. Occupational shifts. Megatrends in society are redefining our world of work. Whereas most people had spent their lives in dedication to industrially based work, post-modern employment centers on information processes.[3] On one hand, this speaks favorably of a literate population that processes new symbol systems and related data. It speaks unfavorably, on the other hand, of the culturally disadvantaged, the unskilled who cannot succeed except with the sweat of their brow. Adult life has and will inalterably continue to change with the move from

2. Martin A. Lang, *Acquiring our Image of God* (Ramsey, N.J.: Paulist Press, 1983).

3. John Naisbitt, *Megatrends* (New York: Warner Books, Inc., 1984).

traditional employment. This dramatic shift, which is presently occurring, will call for new forms of adult ministry—forms that will have to address imaginatively the new life of the literate adult. But, more important, we will have to address the hardships of the disadvantaged adult.

Syntheses

If my assumptions about our present age are correct, then presumably we are faced with an agenda that is neither confrontational nor icono-clastic. But, we must face the facts. Adults have made a megaleap in consciousness that transcends former structures, services, and disci-plines. Modern adults are no less in need of religious services than their predecessors; they are just more discriminating. Today, adults are able to make decisions and come to conclusions about religiously significant issues, with or without us. People today will be heard or they will dismiss us.

The post-modern agenda for adult life is new and challenging. There-fore, we might conclude that the Church's pastoral ministry will be chal-lenged to respond differently to adult members. This call for a changed focus is not an indictment of past practices but a request for an expanded posture and related services. Recall, Rita did not object to Catholic the-ological theory. Rather, she found little of it put into practice.

What more can we do? I suggest that we are being challenged to develop new mind-sets regarding our adult members. Those mind-sets might be described as "stepping out of our Sunday clothes and putting on the apron of service." We are to take our theology into the shopping malls of life. How? The following attitudinal mind-sets for adult ministry make sense to me. They call for healing, reconciling, and affirming min-istries to adults. They are an invitation to readjust our minds so as to adjust our actions.

Adult Ministry

Is this adult education? If we mean a highly technical and structured environment for receiving researched data, no! However, if we under-stand education as a formative ministry, involving adults in the process of self-definition, determination, and spiritual maturation, I would con-cur. The adult ministry being called for is more a state of the heart than of the head. The shape of adult ministry that I propose is a ministry to, with, for, and from adults. It differs from ministry to children because adults differ from children.

Mind-Sets for Ministry to Adults in a Changing World

1. Ministry to adults. Ministry that directs itself to adult needs can best be described as "service oriented." Church organizers responsible for ministry to adults need to recognize adult needs. In light of those factors that differentiate our present world from previous eras, adult ministers are to appreciate the context of the adult's life environment.

Take Rita's situation. Adult life catapulted her into new experiences. She came abreast of expanded needs, spiritual questions related to changes in life's possibilities. In this context, she needed someone in a church-related ministry to assist her—by listening to her questions and directing services related to her spiritual quest.

Ministry *to* adults helps adults assimilate the group life of Catholics; enter into Catholic ritual and worship; identify with the local parochial community; appreciate the faith in the context of life experiences; find forums for self-discovery; meet needs; and seek spiritual counseling.

2. Ministry with adults. Adult educators know that adults learn best in contexts where life experiences are affirmed and peer sharing is possible. Church-related adult ministry relies on this principle. Adults who have at least a nominal interest in the spiritual life can be brought to important insights about faithfulness by being provided opportunities to discover this with their peers. Often, personal crises are tempered by reducing the tension that exists when one thinks a personal/spiritual problem is unique and unshareable. Peer ministry among adults justifies the much heralded "enablement" process. In the practical realm, ministry *with* adults is peer ministry (even without its being recognized as such) that leads adults closer to Christ and to the Church. The process of adults ministering to one another has been happening from time immemorial. Our task is to recognize it, tag it for church service, and support it in our people. Rita found solace with members of the Assembly of God. These believers were convinced that religious and spiritual ministry happens best at the lateral (peer) level. So do I!

3. Ministry for adults. Life's surprises can threaten spiritual wellness. In the context of adult ministry, support systems are to be generated to aid the adult through these difficulties. Consider some key life events: birth, marriage, death. The caring posture of the local faith community speaks volumes about its depth of faith. Are we ready to intervene when the red flags of life are raised? Can we provide solace, sympathy, and sensitivity? When things go wrong for good people, who helps them understand that they are not alone and abandoned by a capricious God? Adult ministry that provides direct assistance puts into concrete terms the baptismal responsibility of the Christian community. If the community is present in times of trouble, it will be invited back in times of joy. The sacramental life makes more sense to adults when Christians themselves demonstrate the symbol of healing in their actions.

4. Ministry from adults. Ministers build on ministry. Once served, one has a natural inclination to be of service. Adults are to be challenged to minister to one another. How is this different from lateral or peer ministry? It is more the generational model, requiring one who is more mature passing on wisdom to the less mature. The parish can call adults into this kind of ministry by eliciting their highest values. Again, take Rita's case. Had other Catholics reached out to Rita, they may have saved her great suffering. We already know how to minister to one another in our families. The Catholic community is an enlarged family. When one suffers, all suffer. Again, as in other cases, adults will offer their services, skills, and talents when they see their peers so inclined.

The State of the Heart

Obviously, the whole premise to this study is centered on the Catholic emotional pulse. Do we have a heart? If so, can we let it show in our ministry to adults?

Look to the Gospels (e.g., Mk 1:40–41; Mt 9:36f; Lk 7:12–13). They are full of heart! Jesus provides spiritual insight into God's kingdom not by theological discourse but by the therapeutic imagery of service. Be healed! Go in peace! Those were his actions. Consider James 2:14–18; the focus is centered on faith-filled action.

Can we pick up on this? I'm convinced we can—and must. The state of the heart in adult ministry is one of hope in the possibilities of adulthood. If we believe God invites us to become full of his grace, then we believe in the potential of that blessing. Our task is to redirect our minds to our hearts and begin to feel for one another. In due time, we will catch on to the greatness our maturity can bring.

Occasionally, when reading a poem or a proverb one's response is, "Exactly!" The poet has managed to describe a thought or feeling that we recognize as our own, but we have never found exactly the right words with which to express ourselves. This same sense of, "Aha! That is exactly my experience," can, and often does, come from group discussions. We refine our own thoughts, our understandings of our experiences, as we discuss them with others. Such an enlightening moment came for me during a conversation that the Region V representatives for adult education had at our three-year gathering in November 1985. The discussion was initially about the recently published vision paper for adult religious education, *Serving Life and Faith: Adult Religious Education and the American Catholic Community*. However, before the discussion was over, we surfaced what were, to me at least, some valuable insights into how one's vision of adult education, one's theoretical basis, affects, for good or ill, the structures and the life spans of parish renewal processes.

Serving Life and Faith takes a very broad view of adult religious education. Paragraph 21 states:

> Although programs in literacy, nutrition, job training, human communications, and the like, do not easily fit into the Church's activity known as catechesis, they are, nonetheless, religious. Here, we use the term, *religion*, in a broad sense. We can say that any activity sponsored by the Christian community that is aimed at attaining human wholeness is religious, and, therefore, the work of the Church. The Church provides her members "the kind of education through which their entire lives can be penetrated with the spirit of Christ, while at the same time she offers her services to all people by way of promoting the full development of the human person, for the welfare of earthly society and the building of a world fashioned more humanly" (*Declaration on Christian Education*, 3).[1]

This view matches the one that the Diocese of Covington adopted in 1980. The *Diocesan Guidelines for Adult Education* say:

Area for Adult Religious Education

The early Church saw three areas in which Christians witnessed to the risen Lord. They are *Kerygma* (message), *Koinonia* (community), and *Diaconia* (service). These three elements form the core elements for all adult religious education.

1. *Kerygma* is concerned with doctrine and Scripture. Suggested topics for adequate adult religious education include (a) Scripture; (b) tradition; (c) liturgy; (d) morality; (e) church history (NCD 185).
2. *Koinonia* is the living faith, community. Adult religious education is concerned with enabling and encouraging adults to develop more fully in faith through and in community: (a) leadership skills; (b) management skills; (c) self-help skills; (d) sharing of abilities and talents; (e) encouraging outreach skills; (f) dealing with the political community.
3. *Diaconia* is witnessing Christ to others in service: (a) preparing liturgical ministers; (b) learning how to visit sick, elderly, unchurched; (c) learning how to care for those who cannot care for themselves; (d) meeting physical, mental, emotional, spiritual needs of community.

Renewal Programs as Adult Religious Education

Margaret N. Ralph

Margaret N. Ralph, Ph.D., is a consultant for Adult Faith Development in the Diocese of Covington.

1. National Advisory Committee on Adult Religious Education, *Serving Life and Faith: Adult Religious Education and the American Catholic Community* (Washington, D.C.: USCC Office of Publishing and Promotion Services, 1986), no. 21.

Since these guidelines were in place before I started working for the Department of Catholic Education, I have been operating with this understanding of adult religious education as long as I have been in the field. For this reason, when I was asked some months ago, "How does your job differ from that of the coordinator for ongoing renewal?" I was unable to answer. All I could say, based on my experience of happy cooperation, was, "Our jobs overlap. We work hand in hand." As I gave that answer, I feared I was missing some crucial distinction. Since our discussion at the regional meeting, I now agree wholeheartedly with it.

It is my experience, and the experience of other adult educators throughout the country, that many of those who work with us in church ministry at the parish level wish to define our tasks more narrowly than we define them ourselves. This difference in vision leads to structural decisions and divisions of tasks that can have far-reaching ramifications in the parish.

The problem can be easily spotlighted by posing the following question: "Is RENEW an example of adult education?" (I use RENEW as an example because it is the renewal process that we have used in our diocese.) The battle that will ensue will clearly delineate a difference in vision among some who work in RENEW and some who work in adult religious education. As an adult educator, my answer is, "Of course. RENEW is an excellent example of adult religious education." I am amazed to hear some from around the country answer, "No, RENEW is much broader than adult education. RENEW is a process, not a program. RENEW is faith sharing, not studying. RENEW has facilitators, not teachers. The goal in RENEW is not knowledge but growth in faith. RENEW encourages people toward action. RENEW is definitely much more than adult education."

Such arguments leave adult educators shaking their heads. Who but adult educators have been laying the foundations for such statements? Adult education is not a program but a process. Adult education involves faith sharing, a reflection on experience, not just head knowledge. Adult education is primarily self-directed—the teacher is not a walking encyclopedia but a fellow pilgrim and facilitator. The goal in adult education is not just to inform but to form, to nurture active adult faith. As one adult educator in our group discussion so aptly put it, "Renewal programs are not examples of virgin births. They were designed on the principles of adult education and now their authors want to disown their own family."

In thinking over the narrow view of adult education that many have, and the fact that some in renewal programs want to disown the title "adult religious education," I am chagrined to admit that some of our problems come from our own practices. The Catholic community in America is barely beginning to live up to the vision of adult religious education presented in *Serving Life and Faith*.

Perhaps, when adult religious educators consider the meaning of adult education, they should consider the parable of the sower. When Jesus spoke of a sower going forth to sow his seed, he described a variety of soils upon which the seed might fall. Obviously, if the seed is to bear fruit, the sower should not only sow the seed but should also do everything possible to help prepare the soil. Whatever helps the soil become more receptive is of crucial concern to the sower. Whatever helps a person whom we are trying to serve become more receptive to the Word is a crucial part of the job of the adult educator. Preparing the soil should include worship, community building, and service. RENEW, through its leadership training, its phone outreach, its integration into the liturgy, its large- and small-group meetings, its take-home materials, its emphasis on evangelization and service, and its ongoing nature, is a good example of "preparing the soil," an excellent model of what adult education should be.

Many adult education programs in the past cannot be compared to the sower and his seed. Rather, they are more like a doctor and his pill. The doctor is healthy, and the patient is sick. The doctor knows what is good for the patient. The doctor doesn't expect the patient to contribute any more than obedience to the healing process. The patient does not have to be receptive, like soil, in order for the seed to bear fruit. Even if he or she simply chokes the pill down, it can have the desired saving effect. While the sower might say, "Be good soil," the doctor need only say, "Swallow this. It's good for you."

How much adult education in the past has been of the "Swallow this. It's good for you," variety? Lectures without dialogue are this kind of education. Memorized answers are this kind of education. Examinations that call for a regurgitation of content taught are this kind of education. Limiting adult education to a one-shot program, or a series of programs unrelated to each other, is this kind of education. How much preparation of the soil have we adult religious educators done? *Serving Life and Faith* may encourage us to become real sowers of the Word. Then, the fact that a process such as RENEW is adult education would be self-evident.

In the meantime, if the leaders of renewal programs and diocesan and parish adult educators could agree that we are all working toward the same goal, namely, adult faith development, the cooperation that would result could have important, practical ramifications on the parish level.

As things now stand, with renewal processes seen not as adult education but as something separate and different, renewal structures in the parishes are formed independently of other parish structures. In many parishes, the renewal structure floats freely, unconnected not only to educational structures but to parish council structures as well. The danger of this lack of connection is that when the original renewal process is over, so may be the ongoing development that the renewal efforts were designed to initiate. If renewal processes are recognized as adult education, and if they are structurally tied to a parish board of education, the chances that the process, so well begun, will survive to bear future fruit are greatly increased. The theory behind renewal affects the parish structures, and the structures affect the viability of the process. Theories have very practical ramifications.

More and more dioceses are using diocesan-wide parish renewal processes. To ensure ongoing growth—fruit a hundredfold—we adult educators who function as doctors must become sowers, and all of us who are trying to sow must come to recognize each other. Those of us who call ourselves adult educators feel related to renewal processes as Adam is to Eve: "You are bone of our bone and flesh of our flesh." Let's realize our unity and reflect that unity in parish structures. Only then will we be able to make ongoing adult faith development, ongoing adult education, ongoing parish renewal a reality. Adult educators have clearly delineated how adults grow in faith. The renewal processes are solidly built on these premises.

This article is about a new ministry formation effort in the Diocese of San Bernardino, California. It is divided into three parts: (1) an outline of our original vision and the first planning efforts; (2) an outline of our current program design and its implications; and, (3) an assessment of the initial construct with evaluative learnings for our readers.

Vision and Planning

Formation efforts during the last twenty years have been for the most part specialization-type courses, identified by their particular content. The liturgy committee attended workshops offered by the diocesan worship office; the parish catechists studied together for their diocesan certification, and so on.

Yet, common to all these individual formation efforts is the parish. It is the parish from which these ministries emerge, and it is the parish to which these ministries contribute.

This interest in parish life has been recognized by the Church in the United States in recent years. The Parish Project, sponsored by the U.S. bishops, studied the characteristics of active parishes throughout the country from 1978 to 1982. In 1980, the Ad Hoc Committee on the Parish issued a vision statement.[1] Currently, the National Pastoral Life Center in New York is doing further research on the parish, and another study is being conducted by the University of Notre Dame.

It was this emphasis on the parish that challenged the authors to explore the implications for ministry formation. The Diocese of San Bernardino has had a strong commitment to ministry formation since its inception in 1979. There is a wide variety of basic and advanced formation programs offered by the individual diocesan ministries. In addition, the Straling Leadership Institute—named after our bishop—was begun in 1980 to respond more fully to the emerging challenge of lay ministry.

This two-year formation experience is designed, first, to call forth from our parishes people who are capable of assuming specific and varied leadership and enabling roles in ministry; second, to provide them with opportunities that are multifaceted and developmental of both the intellect and spirit; and, third, to form a faith community among them by providing opportunities for their sharing and growing together.

As the first graduating classes of the Institute returned to their parishes, we began to hear new needs emerging. The graduates were calling for further insights into the life of the parish. There was also a need to develop additional pastoral skills.

In dialoguing with the graduates, several directions began to take shape: (1) there was a need to focus on parish life as an independent educational goal; (2) there was a need to provide a "rectory window experience" (viewing the parish in totality); most lay ministers enter ministry through a single focus (e.g., liturgy, catechetics); and (3) there was a need for recognizing and addressing skills formation.

To respond to these needs, we began to design a one-year formation experience in the spring of 1983. Feeling that it was an opportunity to build on the process and experience of the first two years, we decided

Pastoral Ministry Formation: A Diocesan Response

Peter R. Bradley and Edna Friedenbach

Peter R. Bradley and Edna Friedenbach co-direct the Pastoral Ministry Formation Program for the Diocese of San Bernardino.

1. Ad Hoc Committee on the Parish, National Conference of Catholic Bishops, *The Parish: A People, A Mission, A Structure* (Washington, D.C.: USCC Office of Publishing and Promotion Services, 1980).

early on to restrict enrollment to graduates of the Institute. The new program is a separate and distinct formation experience and one of several post-Institute opportunities for ongoing study and training.

Our design took the name Pastoral Ministry Formation (PMF) and entailed a fourfold purpose: (1) to study more deeply the role of the Catholic parish by immersing the participants in several aspects of parish life; (2) to provide additional opportunities in pastoral skills formation beyond what was currently available; (3) to provide a broader formation in parish ministry for current ministers (e.g., directors of religious education, youth ministers); (4) to build a foundation for those who are seeking new horizons in parish ministry (e.g., pastoral associate, parish business manager).

The following is an excerpt from the PMF "Philosophy Statement":

> When skills development is integrated into both training in spiritual leadership and methods of theological reflection, it makes a major contribution to professional education in ministry.
>
> The introduction of skills development into ministerial training is related to a significant shift in the understanding of the role of the minister in the community. Today, the minister is seen in a less one-dimensional way, that is, as the sole decision-maker or as the only spiritual guide. Indeed, the initial posture of the minister is that of listener. The minister is called to attend to the faith of the community before acting. The minister reflects in order to act. This reflection follows closely the listening effort.
>
> So, in addition to needing those skills that enable him or her to attend to the texts of Scripture and to the story of church history, the minister must develop a proficiency in listening to people at a meaningful level.
>
> Further, as the minister moves from an authoritarian role in the community, he or she must possess skills that can facilitate appropriate sharing of diverse convictions. Such skills are important for moving the ideal of shared responsibility and collegiality beyond rhetoric and toward practical application.
>
> . . . Finally, because ministry must have visible effects in the faith community, skills in decision making are essential. The minister must be able to move the desires of the *sensum fidelium* to completion . . .
>
> . . . We, in the Diocese of San Bernardino, state clearly that personal skill development is an essential part of our ministry formation, along with community building and theological education. . . .

Program Design

Our current design is now in its second generation. Needless to say, we learned a great deal from our first experience. The design features multiple components, each addressing a particular learning need. The components are (1) a monthly, one-day session with a facilitator, who develops a specific topic area; (2) a regular faith-sharing session; (3) a time to experience new parish ministries/issues/people (pastoral experience component); (4) an introduction to *The Parish Self-Study Guide*[2]; (5) a pastoral evaluation project; (6) a mentor experience with an established parish minister; (7) resource development including a session text, handouts, audio-visual, bibliographies.

2. Ad Hoc Committee on the Parish, National Conference of Catholic Bishops, *The Parish Self-Study Guide* (Washington, D.C.: USCC Office of Publishing and Promotion Services, 1982).

I will further develop each component so that the goal, the process, and the content of each are clear.

1. Monthly Session

Each session, using lived experience, church tradition, and cultural information, takes a particular area of importance to pastoral ministry and engages the participants in ministerial reflection.

The actual flow for the year looks like this:

September: *What is Pastoral Ministry?* covers parish vision and models, identifies the uniqueness of pastoral ministry, and provides a method for theological reflection in ministry.

October: *Cultural Sensitivity in Ministry* covers the value of cultural traditions and ethnicity in our church experience.

November: *Pastoral Leadership* covers styles of leadership and helps participants to identify their leadership styles.

December: *Pastoral Care* offers an introduction to the principles of pastoral care and the helping skills, and emphasizes the difference between pastoral care and pastoral counseling.

January: *Retreat Experience* is a weekend getaway focusing on the participants and their call to ministry.

A Tract System is in effect for the next three months. There are two areas of interest: Parish Administration and Pastoral Care. Participants choose one on which to focus.

Pastoral Administration Tract	Pastoral Care Tract
February	**February**
Pastoral Planning	*Christian Life Patterns*
• covers the value of pastoral planning in ministry	• explains normal Christian life changes and faith development
• participants work through several different models of planning	• compares the life patterns of male and female Christians
	• provides a process to motivate changes in participants' lives that can be used to motivate change in others
	• explores family systems with drug and/or alcohol dependencies

March

Parish Administration

- covers the value of church administration as a ministry

- provides models of parish hospitality

- reviews Christian management and accountability systems

- introduces the role of computers in parish life

March

Pastoral Care #2

- explores the pastoral care function by comparing historical and contemporary expressions of healing, sustaining, guiding, and reconciling

- uses role playing, film and tape experiences to enable participants to "put on" the feelings, words, and body language of the counselee

- uses verbatims and reflective processes to help the pastoral care person discern his or her own feelings and reactions to the counselee

April

New Ministries Sharing

- a seminar with lay ministers who are serving as pastoral associates and parish business managers and their pastors

April

Pastoral Care #3

- uses a pastoral care team as a resource to share their actual experiences of crisis counseling

- provides a background for understanding the stages of death and dying

- explores how the death and dying process is present in any loss situation

- gives each participant feedback from a pastoral care team about the situations they have recorded in their verbatims

- explores how the individual seeking care is part of a family system; reviews how family systems are affected by crisis

In May, the two tracts come back together.

May: *Team Ministry* covers the theology and working models of team ministry.

June: *Closing* offers a day of reflection, evaluation, and celebration.

2. Faith Sharing

Our faith-sharing component is very special to us. It actually begins back in the Straling Leadership Institute, where each participant belongs to a small faith-sharing group for two years. The groups move through a series of twenty-five sessions, under the leadership of a trained facilitator. We believe strongly that each minister must not only be in touch with his or her own faith story but also must be able to listen for the presence of the Lord in others' stories.

The faith-sharing segments in Pastoral Ministry Formation are approximately three hours in length. The participants are divided into small groups by geographic regions through a simple discernment process on the opening weekend. The responsibility for scheduling, hospitality, and facilitation is rotated among the members of each group. The topics relate to the monthly sessions, with the design of the faith-sharing process provided by our office.

3. Pastoral Experience Component

Because many lay ministers entered parish ministry through a specialty, such as religious education, there are significant areas of parish life with which they may be unfamiliar. Each participant is encouraged to spend three to four hours a month investigating these new areas. A simple reflection sheet was developed to assist the participants with capturing their insights and feelings. It asks two questions: How do you feel about the experience? What did you learn from the experience?

4. The Parish Self-Study Guide

Our Diocesan Parish Visitation Program utilizes *The Parish Self-Study Guide* as a means for the parish to prepare for the bishop's arrival. Our use of the self-study guide brought the participants into constructive dialogue with their pastors. It also allowed the participants to explore unfamiliar areas of parish life.

5. Pastoral Evaluation Project

This aspect of the program affords the trainee with an opportunity to engage in an in-depth evaluation of his or her present ministry. We found that many lay ministers had not experienced the benefits of an evaluation process of this nature and greatly appreciated what they learned from having done it. The participants dedicated themselves to completing the evaluation forms fully and honestly and were quite willing to share openly their findings in a group.

6. Mentor Experience

One issue that has surfaced for us in lay ministry is the lack of role models. We attempt to address this need in PMF by connecting each participant with a parish minister who is a Pastoral Ministry Formation graduate, has an effective ministry role, and has prolonged experience in the ministry. They meet four times a year, with preliminary resource material distributed prior to each meeting. The meetings allow the participants to integrate the various components of Pastoral Ministry Formation through discussion with the mentor. Very often, these discussions lead from PMF issues to other concerns of the participant.

7. Resource Development

We attempt to provide a well-rounded collection of resource materials that will be useful long after the participants leave PMF. We also keep in touch with new developments as they arise. Recently, a parish in our diocese produced an entire packet of parish orientation materials (e.g., brochure, ministry listings, parish yellow pages). We obtained a copy of that packet for each participant because of its unique pastoral dimension.

Assessment

We began our first year with sixteen people and graduated thirteen. Three participants left because of personal and work reasons. A surprise was the makeup of our group. We had expected ministers who were basically volunteers, contributing five to seven hours per week to their parish. Instead, the majority of our first group were full-time paid parish ministers. There were three DREs, one RCIA minister, one parish secretary, one parish administrative assistant, two parish business managers, and one Catholic school teacher. The rest of the people covered a range of parish ministries: religious education, hospital ministry, young adult ministry, and ministry to the elderly.

At the last session, we evaluated our first year. The following issues surfaced:

Positive	*Negative*
• time to connect • calibre of instructors • tapped into personal gifts • faith-sharing was vital • learned and developed pastoral skills • excellent resources	• too much material in one-day session • texts not always given in advance • need to respond to particular ministries (this was addressed by introducing the two-track system) • *The Parish Self-Study Guide* could not be completed without parish cooperation • start pastoral project earlier

For those readers who are currently involved in pastoral ministry training or may be considering such a beginning, we offer several insights based on our experience.

1. Training components should complement each other in ways that provide strong, holistic experiences. Mentoring, faith sharing, and new parish experiences added important dimensions to the typical six-hour classroom workshop.

2. A working relationship with other diocesan offices is a must. Their resources need to be part of your experience.
3. Try to build upon the participants' previous training experiences; avoid beginning from square one.
4. By affirming the participants' current knowledge and skills and introducing them to learning areas that are practical and immediately usable, you will greatly improve their self-confidence when they are back in their parishes.
5. Be sure to use the talents present in the class; for instance, a participant in our first group left her desk as a learner to lead the parish computer section during the Parish Administration course. We are truly all co-learners.
6. Different ministry specialties can be effectively accommodated in the same program by using a tracking system.

We look forward with excitement to each group in Pastoral Ministry Formation. We believe now more than ever that the ministry in the parish requires special attention to the uniqueness of parish life in the Roman Catholic Church tradition. It will only grow and develop as we move closer to the 1990s.

Anyone interested in finding out more about our new program is welcome to contact us. Also, we are eager to learn about other similar programs throughout the country. Write: Pastoral Ministry Formation, 6948 Elmwood Road, San Bernardino, CA 92404.

Adult Learning, the RCIA, and the Black Catholic

Greer G. Gordon

Those of us who work with the RCIA find no difficulty whatsoever in seeing the intimate relationship between spirituality and the RCIA. In fact, we could very well say that the RCIA has no meaning unless it draws upon the fullness of the community's spiritual legacy. However, we often fail to see the necessity of using sound catechetical methodology in our approach to the catechumenate.

Most of us rely upon the styles of teaching we were once subjected to, often trying to teach the Word rather than share the Word. As a result, the "speaking of the Word of the Lord in a manner in which it can be heard" (catechesis) is oftentimes approached as an exercise in scriptural reflection, with very little sharing of the content of the Word and the faith. As such, we attempt to share the Word of the Lord in much the same fashion as we attempt to catechize children, namely, using methods that respect neither the life experiences nor the learning preferences of catechumens.

Frequently, we use methods that require a literacy level that even the director of the program may not have. What do we do, then, when a nonliterate adult asks to join our faith community? Since all are welcome, not just the literate, it is imperative that those who work with the RCIA have a sound understanding of adult religious education.

Notably, it is helpful for them to understand three basic principles of adult learning: (1) adults bring with them a wealth of life experiences that must be respected and integrated with their quest for God; (2) adults need freedom to question and to respond to what is being shared with them; (3) adults need to feel that they are respected as mature individuals who are recognized as being equal to those who are facilitating their learning.

Life Experience

Adults bring with them into the learning forum a wealth of life experiences. They have known the joys and the sorrows of life. They have lived with the devastating effects of racism and other forms of prejudice. As black people, they have been reared with an astute sense of God, as the God of history, "who not only saved Israel, but also me." These adults come into the RCIA with a personal salvation history, a deeply personal experience of God, which has brought them to the doors of this faith community. During this time of formation, they need to be encouraged to reflect upon the experiences of their lives in the light of the Gospel—identifying the areas of life and death in them; looking at those aspects of who they are that are good and those aspects of who they are that are not good and need to change. In other words, they need to be encouraged to listen to God as they reflect upon how God has been present throughout their lives. This draws the adult into a more intuitive style of sharing, moving from the interior of the person to the realities immediately around them.

The intuitive style of learning is, generally speaking, a preferred mode of operation for black people. The power of intuition is a deeply interior sensing, which is the primary means by which black people come

Greer G. Gordon is former assistant director of Adult Religious Education/ Formation in the Archdiocese of Washington and a member of the Carmelite Community, Baltimore, Maryland.

to know and understand. It is, as such, an abstract way of perceiving reality. Those who are more inclined to use concrete and exterior ways of perception are oftentimes confused by the highly intuitive person. For this reason, it is very important that those who would journey with the adults in the RCIA process be cognizantly open to the experiences of others. They must be able to affirm their experiences, even if they have not had similar ones. This is particularly important where the facilitator of the process is not black or is a black person who comes from a different subculture within the black community. Perhaps, it is helpful to remember that affirmation of the shared experiences of another is the same as affirming the one who shares the experiences. The life experiences of adults really form the core content of their lives. Thus, to fully acknowledge the individual person, the facilitator must be willing to acknowledge the value of that particular adult's life experiences.

Free to Speak

Adults need freedom to question and to respond to the concepts that are shared with them. They need to feel that they can freely agree, or disagree, with what is presented. Facilitators of adult learning often state that they want the participants to feel free to take issue with them; however, the signals that they give may make the adults feel that their reactions are not at all welcome. Often, too, the facilitator, who is presented as the "authority" on the subject, takes questions as if they are insults to his or her intelligence. When this happens, the average adult learner feels highly uncomfortable.

A learning environment such as this most assuredly violates the black adult's tendency toward emotiveness in the learning forum. The vast majority of black adults tend to be highly emotive in the manner in which they respond to reality. Thus, they need to be able to affirm what is being said as true, or they need to be able to question it on the basis of its not being true in their life experiences. In either case, the purpose is the movement toward clarity and truth. A learning forum that does not encourage the quest for truth is certainly not geared toward the sharing of faith.

Dignity of the Person

Adults need to feel that they are respected as mature individuals who are recognized as being equal to those who are facilitating their learning. Oftentimes, adults can be made to feel that their lack of knowledge makes them less full members of the community than others; that their lack of knowledge of particular teachings of the Church or their lack of certain academic credentials makes them unequal to some. The unfortunate fact is that this attitude is often conveyed by those who would call themselves "ministers" within the Church.

The faith of Jesus says that all are welcome and all are equal. It would appear that those who would share the faith need to be sensitive to honoring Christ's presence in each individual. For, it is the image of God in us that makes us all one in Christ's love. No matter what our age, race, or level of education, we are all called by Christ to come to the waters of new life.

So it is that those who would be engaged in the catechetical dimensions of the RCIA need to have a more sensitive and clearly articulated understanding of whom the adult is and the principles of adult learning that effectively govern the affective sharing of faith.

IV. RESOURCES

Proclaiming the Gospel is a perennial task and joy for the Church of Jesus Christ. Rarely if ever has it been more pressing a need, more urgent a duty, and more ennobling a vocation than in these times when mankind stands poised between unprecedented fulfillment and equally unprecedented calamity.[1]

These words, taken from the bishops' 1972 pastoral message on education, *To Teach as Jesus Did*, have a special urgency in 1986 as humanity continues to risk calamity. Adult educators must accept the challenge to proclaim the gospel by offering substantive programs that provide an opportunity to apply gospel values to contemporary issues.

Never has there been a more propitious time. The issues of today are complex, and people are searching for answers to questions raised by these issues. Our educated society offers ample opportunity to become informed on real estate, gourmet cooking, and wine tasting, but it offers fewer opportunities to examine the root causes of hunger, racism, and human rights. The Church needs to fill this void. The Church should help shape beliefs and values; it should help search for solutions to the pressing problems of society. By providing a forum for study, discussion, and decision making, adult educators enable church members to assist in building the Kingdom of God.

As people become more informed on issues such as homelessness, the farm problem, and environmental concerns, they will become more aware that people of faith have a basic responsibility to the poor and to those injured by unjust structures. Media coverage of the situation in South Africa and of the struggle for freedom in the war-torn countries of Central America has brought the effects of injustice and oppression into our living rooms.

As communication makes the world smaller, people are becoming aware that humanity is linked—that the global village is a reality. Decisions' made in living rooms, in churches, in corporate board rooms, and in the halls of Congress affect people at the local, national, and international levels.

The National Conference of Catholic Bishops has declared in its pastoral letters, *The Challenge of Peace: God's Promise and Our Response* and *Catholic Social Teaching and the U.S. Economy*, that our defense and economic policies have more than political implications. They raise moral questions to which the Church must respond; indeed, it has responded. Through encyclicals and other church documents, Catholic religious leaders continue to influence the secular world. Since 1891, eleven other major church documents on peace and justice have been issued. In 1971, the Synod of Bishops' Second General Assembly made the following statement: "Action on behalf of justice and participation in the transformation of the world fully appear to us to be a constitutive dimension of the preaching of the Gospel or, in other words, of the Church's mission for the redemption of the human race and its liberation from every oppressive situation."

Action on behalf of justice is not an option meant only for a few activists while others go about their daily activities. Social analysis is not a contemporary buzzword. Ministry for justice is the basic responsibility

Building the Kingdom of God

Mary Lou Durall

Mary Lou Durall is the director of Leaven, Silver Spring, Maryland.

1. National Conference of Catholic Bishops, "To Teach as Jesus Did," in *Pastoral Letters of the United States Catholic Bishops*, Hugh J. Nolan, ed. (Washington, D.C.: United States Catholic Conference Office of Publishing and Promotion Services, 1983), vol. III, 307.

of all Christians, and all people are accountable for the way this justice dimension is present in their lives. So, too, are our churches and institutions. Even more important, they have the power base to bring about real systemic change.

In 1973, the United States Catholic Conference, in a statement issued on the twenty-fifth anniversary of the Universal Declaration of Human Rights said, "Catholics should be in the forefront of those speaking in defense of and acting for the fulfillment of the rights of men and women at the local, national, and international levels. Our commitment to these goals should be expressed personally and institutionally in the policies and programs the Church sponsors and supports in society."[2]

Adult educators can be of special service to the Church and to society by offering institutional programs that encourage parishioners to speak on their own behalf and that of others. Our churches should become centers for justice and peace education by offering programs to help people link faith and justice.

Leaven, a social justice education curriculum in Spanish and English, does just that—it links faith and justice. Developed by the Sisters of Mercy of the Union in 1984, *Leaven* provides an opportunity to discuss economic, social, cultural, and political problems and to make informed moral decisions on these issues. Developed for small-group discussion, *Leaven* is easy to use, takes no lesson plans, and is designed so that the group leader need not have a special knowledge of justice issues or training in facilitation. The materials come with prayers and scripture passages designed around each topic and with an introduction that includes hints on setting up successful groups. The twelve units include *Leaven* Changes; Human Rights; Poverty and Affluence; United States Culture in the 1980s; Conflict Management through Listening; Racism: Two Americas; War and Peace; Structural Analysis; Sexism and Human Liberation; Global Limits; Change in a Democratic Society; *Leaven* Alive!

Each *Leaven* unit can be used in a two-hour session. The units encourage sharing of experiences. Participants in *Leaven* groups have written to say: "*Leaven* has been an enlightening and challenging series for myself and all the Mississippi participants. It has been easy to facilitate . . ."; "*Leaven* has led to a group bonding I wouldn't have believed possible. I will recommend it to the head of lay ministry training in our diocese"; "As a result of *Leaven*, I've been more aware of social injustices. It's inspired me to take part in other organizations along these lines."

Leaven was written by Sr. Loretta Carey, RDC, director of the Fordham/NCEA Regional Center for Education for Justice & Peace in New York City and Sr. Kathleen Kanet, RSHM, director of the School Program at the Intercommunity Center for Justice and Peace in New York City. The materials were intended for the "person in the pew"—as an introduction to social analysis. A follow-up unit to apply the concepts of social change to local issues is included.

The *Leaven* units move participants from functioning primarily on the personal and interpersonal levels to thinking about change on the structural level. The units teach how to analyze social problems and work to make changes where injustices exist. The process allows people to

2. Ibid., 386.

discuss controversial problems without becoming angry with one another. The materials link people working in advocacy and those doing direct service.

Leaven is recommended for groups of five to twelve people who want to spend an evening discussing contemporary issues and for people interested in real social change. The program is excellent for lay leadership development, Advent and Lent studies, youth and adult education classes, as well as renewal and encuentro groups. Groups that use it report few dropouts.

Margaret Mead on her deathbed said that the survival of civilization would depend, not on government and bureaucracies, but on "citizen volunteer associations, gathering together, deepening and growing together, and going out and taking social action."

More and more people are joining groups at the grass-roots level to speak collectively against the ills of society, and local groups are joining other groups to become national voices in the peace movement.

Churches, too, are finding that small groups, growing together, form the foundation of a strong parish life. The *Leaven* materials can foster this community building and provide the background out of which parish service programs and volunteer associations develop. These groups working together can make a difference in the lives of the people in the local community and in the global community.

The *Leaven* materials help answer questions on how the Church should relate to major contemporary social problems and how the Church communicates social justice values to its members. For more information, write: *Leaven*, 1320 Fenwick Lane, #610, Silver Spring, MD 20910; telephone: (301) 587-6310.

Feeding the Hunger: The Center for Spiritual Development

Ann Marie Wallace

The Center for Spiritual Development of the Archdiocese of New York has as its mission the development and implementation of programs and services to facilitate the spiritual growth and development of the people of the archdiocese. It is a response to the growing hunger of people for a deeper spiritual life. Begun in 1979 at the inspiration of Terence Cardinal Cooke, the center is located on the grounds of Blessed Sacrament Monastery, Yonkers, New York. Cardinal Cooke believed that the prayers of the monastery's cloistered Sacramentine Nuns would be highly important to the center's success.

For the first four years of its existence, the center was devoted exclusively to the spiritual development of the laity and was so named. Under the direction of Fr. Bruce Nieli, CSP, assisted by Fr. John Budwick and Sr. Dolores Harrison, PBVM, the center offered programs of study and prayer for parish leaders and those involved in ministry. It also gave staff service to the spirituality movements in the archdiocese, such as Cursillo, Charismatic Renewal, Marriage Encounter, and youth programs, including those for black and Hispanic youth. The center also responded to invitations from parishes, schools, and other organizations for days and evenings of prayer and for retreats. In 1980, it launched RENEW, which involved several parishes in a three-year renewal program.

In 1983, following Fr. Nieli's appointment to a Paulist Mission Team in Texas, Fr. Anthony Ciorra, OFM Cap., became codirector of the center with Fr. Budwick. Renamed the Center for Spiritual Development, it became the base for two other offerings in spirituality that were already operational: The School of Spirituality, directed by Fr. Ciorra, and the Spiritual Direction Referral Service, coordinated by Sr. Patricia Lally, OP.

The center offers the following services:

- The School of Spirituality
- Annual Spirituality Convocation
- Spiritual Direction Referral Service
- Ministering to Ministers
- Programs for Parish Renewal
- Spirituality Resources
- *TIDINGS*, the Center Newsletter

The School of Spirituality

The School offers three programs of study: The Spiritual Direction Program; The Spiritual Development Program; and A Journey through Scripture.

The Spiritual Direction Program is a two-year program to prepare priests, religious, and laity for the ministry of spiritual direction.

The course of study includes courses in psychological and spiritual growth and development; the literature of Christian spirituality; the skills and processes of spiritual direction; and seminars on topics related to direction: prayers, discernment, justice and peace issues, dreams, and the use of guided imagery in meditation. Group and individual super-

Ann Marie Wallace, Ph.D., is the director of the Center for Spiritual Development in the Archdiocese of New York.

vision is part of the second-year program. In addition to the thirty weeks of classes, the first-year students experience a guided prayer weekend and a communication-skills workshop. The second-year students are supervised in directing the prayer of others during a weekend retreat and attend a two-day workshop on sexual issues in spiritual direction. A certificate is offered at the satisfactory completion of the program.

This program began in 1974 when, at the request of Cardinal Cooke, Fr. Benedict J. Groeschel, OFM Cap., taught a course for priest confessors at St. Joseph Seminary, Dunwoodie. The following year, he started a thirty-week, ninety-hour program in spiritual direction and religious counseling, open to religious and laity, as well. In 1977, it moved to Blessed Sacrament Monastery, and by 1978 it was a two-year program. Increasing interest, especially among the laity, necessitated an evening session to accommodate those who were eager to learn more about the spiritual journey. In 1980, the second year of the program provided two courses of study, one for spiritual direction and one for the development of the new population of laity and religious.

The Spiritual Development Program is a two-year program for those who seek to know God more deeply and to work more intensely for the coming of the kingdom. Its focus is on growth in one's relation to God and on sharing the fruits of that relationship with families, friends, fellow parishioners, and religious communities. The first year of the program offers courses in spiritual and psychological growth and development; peer counseling and faith sharing; and the foundations of the Christian life (i.e., ecclesiology, Christology, sacraments, morality, and selected documents of Vatican II). The second year provides courses in helping skills, spirituality and the call to discipleship, and the New Testament.

This program seems to be a viable response to the hunger of laity and religious for a deepening spiritual life and for an updating of their religious education in terms of Vatican II. This program takes place at six locations throughout the archdiocese: Manhattan, Yonkers, and Staten Island; and Westchester, Dutchess, and Rockland counties. Over 400 students are enrolled, ranging in age from the twenties through the sixties.

A Journey through Scripture was started at the center in Yonkers, and at the Marian Shrine, West Haverstraw, by Fr. Ciorra to address both the desire of people since Vatican II to learn more about Scripture and the fundamentalism sometimes found in prayer groups. This is a two-year program in bible study, with one year devoted to the Old Testament and one year to the New Testament. Two-hour classes meet for twenty weeks each year. A third course opened in 1986 at the Catholic Center in Manhattan and is cosponsored by the archdiocesan catechetical office.

Annual Spirituality Convocation

The first annual Spirituality Convocation was initiated in 1985 in recognition of the desire of people to deepen continually their knowledge and experience of the spiritual life. In addition to featured speakers, workshops on a variety of current topics in spirituality are also offered.

The first two convocations attracted an average of 1,500 priests, religious, and laity from the tri-state area and beyond.

Spiritual Direction Referral Service

Established in 1978 as a part-time service connected with the Spiritual Direction Program, it became a component of the center in 1983. Its purpose is to assist the many priests, religious, and laity who express difficulty in finding a suitable director. Drawing on a resource list of qualified directors—both graduates of the Spiritual Direction Program and others—Sr. Patricia Lally, OP, has been coordinating this service from its inception. She interviews each person who seeks a director and recommends one with the appropriate background and accessibility to the directee. At times, the person seeking direction may need counseling. After discussing this with the individual, she can recommend accordingly, either to individual counselors or to the Family Consultation Service of the archdiocese, which offers counseling for religious and priests, as well as laity.

Ministering to Ministers

The increasing spiritual needs of people result in increasing demands on priests, religious, and laity who, in turn, need to refresh themselves to avoid burnout and to continue to be life-giving to others. The center offers services for priests, religious, and ministerial groups, as well as continuing education for spiritual directors.

For members of the clergy, the center, which is cosponsored by the Office of Spirituality, will provide lists of priests and others who can direct days of prayer and reflection for the vicariate area conferences.

Three services are provided for religious: (1) Mornings of reflection and reconciliation for religious brothers and sisters provide opportunities in various locations throughout the archdiocese to experience the sacrament of reconciliation in an atmosphere of prayer and reflection. The morning includes a short conference, time for silent reflection and the opportunity for individual reception of the sacrament. (2) Days or evenings of recollection for local communities are offered in a format that includes a presentation, quiet time, media, and optional sharing. (3) Resource people are available to facilitate local community goal setting and evaluation.

For those on pastoral teams or for people in similar ministries, days of prayer can be arranged at the center or in a place chosen by the group. Individuals may come to the center for private days of prayer when there are no scheduled activities.

Programs for Parish Renewal

The center offers RENEW and Beyond RENEW, *A Call to More*, days of prayer for laity, and the At Home Retreat Program.

The three-year cycle of RENEW has been completed in over ninety parishes throughout the archdiocese, with new ones becoming involved. Many parishes have continued into the Beyond RENEW phase, and the center provides material and other services as needed.

A Call to More was developed in response to the many parishes requesting renewal or prayer experiences for particular groups. It also serves as a ministerial opportunity for the graduates of the School of Spirituality. *A Call to More* is a program prepared on a specific theme by a team of resource people and presented by the staff and trained graduates. It includes talks, group discussions, a media presentation, and prayer services. The program is flexible and can take place over an entire day or in an evening. A booklet that is given to each participant includes the prayer services and scripture references on one of two themes available for further prayer and reflection: *Compassion* and *Reconciliation*.

Two days of prayer are scheduled for the laity at the center, and groups or individuals can arrange similar days at other times. Center facilities now include a chapel.

On alternate years, the center cosponsors the At Home Retreats Training Program with At Home Retreats International. This program trains parish leaders to conduct the At Home Retreat: a thirteen-week experience based on the spiritual exercises of St. Ignatius for small groups in a parish or other community setting.

Spirituality Resources

At the center, we have become aware of three important things: (1) The needs of people in the archdiocese as individuals and groups are many and varied. (2) There is no way in which our staff of three people can address all those needs. (3) There are many religious, priests, and laity who have training and experience in spirituality but for a variety of reasons cannot work in this area full time. Many would welcome occasional opportunities to do so, but they need a base of operation.

Thus, we have concluded that the center could provide the networking that connects needs with resources.

The center is also developing a library of printed and audio-visual materials on prayer, spirituality, Scripture, the spiritual development process, and related topics.

Through our newsletter, *TIDINGS*, we invited people who have training and experience in spirituality to become resource people for our center, and we have been most gratified by their caliber and by their number—over fifty to date.

TIDINGS is published three times a year and publicizes the programs and services of the center.

Conclusion

The existence of the center is based on the recognition of the hunger in people for a personal relationship with God that pours itself out in the love and service of others. People are also anxious to respond to the challenges of Vatican II, which recognized that the responsibility to build the Kingdom belongs to all the baptized People of God, not just to a select few. It is important for the laity to engage in this task out of a Christian spirituality that is understood and lived.

One of the great strengths of the programs, especially in the Spiritual Direction and Spiritual Development Programs, is the attempt to integrate the traditional principles of Christian asceticism and mysticism with the insights of contemporary psychology. Many of the faculty of those programs have degrees in both psychology/counseling and spirituality or theology.

In the development of programs and services, we take a somewhat responsive stance. We try to listen to needs and to "fill the hungry." During the past year, the staff engaged in eight consultations with the staffs from archdiocesan ministries offices to listen to their needs, insights, and suggestions. Included were offices that deal with catechetics; family life; religious; substance abuse ministry; health and hospitals; pastoral life; youth ministry. In addition, we met with the director of the Church Leadership Program at Fordham. The staff will meet with others this year.

The staff is composed of one director, two associate directors, and a secretary. We try to keep a prayerful atmosphere at the center and recite Daytime Prayer together when we can. Each staff member engages in the ministry of spiritual direction along with the center's other works.

The composition of the staff reflects the emerging collaboration and cooperation of priest, religious, and laity in the work of the Church. The faculty of the School of Spirituality mirrors the same reality, as do the resource people.

Our greatest strength is, I think, in our vision of the Church, which invites all the baptized to mission both to the People of God and to the world through the power of the indwelling Spirit. Our task is to empower others for mission.

In this future-shock society, where the world scene can change from day to day, people need to be rooted deeply in the vine that is Christ in order to respond effectively to the constant change that can so easily be overwhelming. It is our hope that, in some small way, we can help them to do this.

For more information about the center and its work, please contact: Ann Marie Wallace, Director, The Center for Spiritual Development, 10 Flagg Street, P.O. Box 44, Yonkers, NY 10703; Phone: (914) 963-5757.

When a four-year-old feels free to express that "Daddy doesn't listen when I talk to him," and a husband is able to share with his wife that he "wants to be something more than the wage earner for his family," and a teenager is able to admit that she "wants her freedom but also wants to belong to her family," and together they create ways to right what's wrong, deepen what's meaningful, and discover and implement new ways in which to grow as family, probably they've been participating in a Family Cluster.

The Family Cluster was founded in 1970 by Margaret Sawin, Ed.D. Since then, it has become one of the best known forms of family enrichment in all faiths and denominations throughout the North American continent. "Family enrichment is the process of enriching or deepening the strengths and attributes which a family already possesses in order to provide further growth and fulfillment for its family members, as well as for the family unit as a whole."[1] Family therapist, Virginia Satir, says that the growth model of learning is based on the notion that a person's behavior changes through transactions with other people. The assumption is that growth and change are positive and energy producing for further growth. The theological message is one of hope and promise.

"The Family Cluster model is an educational mode of learning for well-functioning families and, therefore, is not therapy nor counseling. These modalities are based on the medical model of pathology and sickness. Enrichment is based on the educational model of normal development and learning."[2]

To the wider field of family enrichment, the contributions of the Family Cluster model are (1) to develop a support group for families in which they can grow and receive caring; (2) to enable families to work on their own concerns, questions, hopes, problems, and dreams in order to develop more awareness and self-direction; (3) to allow for celebration and worship of the in-depth experiences of life; (4) to teach skills to family members so that they are enabled to live together more harmoniously.

While the nature of the Family Cluster model is intergenerational, one of its primary purposes is to be an environment for the growth of adults. Recognizing as we do today the importance of the earliest stages of human life for the future realization of the whole person, the Family Cluster model provides an effective means for the formative years to be nurtured in support of lifelong learning and the personal growth called for in adult education, especially adult religious education.

"A Family Cluster is a group of four or five complete family units which contract to meet together periodically over an extended period of time for shared educational experiences related to their living in relationship within their families. A cluster provides mutual support, training in skills which facilitate the family living in relationship, and celebration of their life and beliefs together."[3]

Family Cluster was a forerunner in considering the family unit as made up of persons who live in relationship with one another, including those who live in the same household; a single person who lives alone but has relationships with others; a couple without children; a one-parent family; and the nuclear family. This broad base is not an adaptation to

Family Clusters: An Environment for Adult Growth

Joseph Crisafulli

Joseph Crisafulli is the director of Adult Religious Education and the Catechumenate in the Diocese of Syracuse.

1. Margaret Sawin, *Family Enrichment with Family Clustering* (Valley Forge, Pa.: Judson Press, 1979), Preface.

2. Ibid.

3. Ibid., 27.

the times but is the heart of authentic family: living in relationship. It is Family Cluster's appropriateness for our times—in particular, the diversity and innovativeness of life styles—that makes it an effective environment for growth. It is also a good vehicle for ministry to singles, marrieds, divorced and separated, widowed and elderly, teenagers and children. The norm for entrance into a Family Cluster is the actual relationship in which one lives.

Those in adult and family ministries should note that it is the *system of the family*, itself, not a model, that provides the intensive framework for growth and change. Because their relationships set the terms, the participants have a good sense of ownership of the process. "Each family system is affirmed for what it is, each is encouraged to change and grow, and each is supported in the new behaviors it tries."[4]

The Family Cluster model's basic goals are

- to provide an intergenerational group of family units where children and adults can relate easily to one another;
- to provide a group that can grow in support and mutuality for all its members;
- to provide a group where parents can gain perspective about their own children through contact with other children and other adults' perceptions of their children; likewise, where children can gain perspectives about their own parents through contact with other parents and other children's perceptions of their parents;
- to provide an opportunity for families to consider experiences seriously related to themselves as individuals, as family members, as group members, and as members of a faith community;
- to provide a group wherein there is opportunity for families to model for each other aspects of their family systems in communication, decision making, interrelating, problem solving, etc.;
- to provide an experience between generations where adults can share their concerns regarding the meaning of life amidst rapid social changes and the aberration of traditional values, and children can deal with their experiences, using the group to help assess them in an atmosphere of support and shared values;
- to help families discover and develop their strengths through increased loving, caring, joy, and creativity;
- to provide an opportunity for positive intervention into family systems so as to facilitate their living and growing together more productively.[5]

Family Cluster's theoretical basis flows from the following five synthesizing concepts:

1. "The *system of the family* provides the most forceful structure for growth and change. Each family is an interwoven group of human components . . ." that ". . . provide reciprocal relationships to each other and to the family as a group."[6] Exposing all family members together to a learning situation subjects each person to the influence of each other's perspectives as well as to that of the family as a whole.

4. Ibid., 30.
5. Ibid., 30–31.
6. Ibid., 31.

84

2. Group dynamics involve the participants in *intra*family and *inter*family exchange, often helping the cluster group to become like an extended family. The manner in which leadership is exerted, indeed shared, is a powerful force in group modeling.

3. As a *growth* model or a *change* model, Family Cluster "facilitates movements toward the actualizing of a family's strengths and potential."[7] This expresses a conviction about each person's uniqueness and desire to grow toward the fulfillment of his or her potential. The result offers each family system more options and choices in response to a fast-changing world.

4. The cluster process, itself, promotes *experiential education.* "Reflected experience rather than didactic content becomes the core of the learning activity."[8] Because it is applicable to all age groups, experiential learning is particularly relevant to faith learning. And, with all the family members present, there is greater opportunity for back-home realization.

5. Cluster experience is based on *process theology.* This means that the belief process is facilitated through individual experiences that are valid and authentic for each person. Process theology recognizes that *all* life's experiences can have religious meaning. This cannot be overemphasized: the framing of our belief styles, content, valuation, and continuous growth are formed within our family relationships. What becomes our family style relates directly to our faith style and stages whether in an affirming or a reactive way.

A variety of events make up the Family Cluster.

A *Family Cluster Training Laboratory* is a training experience that includes several variables: a week-long residential setting with families organized into clusters; a number of skillshops for learning skills and theory related to the model (human interaction skills, design/planning skills, family systems understanding, group dynamics, leadership, and other related skills). Trainees lead cluster sessions and receive supervision from skilled staff persons. The lab builds total community among all present: family members, trainees, and staff.

A lab is composed around three program tracks:

1. *Family Clusters.* A lab may have two or three clusters, of five or six families each, meeting twice a day and exposed to a wide range of experiences. Families may attend a lab for the Family Cluster experience without a member of the family being in the training track.

2. *Persons-in-Training.* These are trainees interested in learning to lead Family Cluster groups. They participate in the cluster sessions with families and, in addition, participate in the skillshops. It is helpful for persons-in-training to have had some background in human relations work, group work, and experiential education. The most helpful asset is an open mind and a spirit of commitment to the process. Not all trainees are ready to lead clusters at the close of the lab.

7. Ibid., 32.
8. Ibid., 33.

85

3. *Leaders of the Clusters and Skillshops*. These are persons experienced in the areas facilitated, and they are always present in each cluster and skillshop.

A *Family Cluster Training Workshop* is a thirty-hour (minimum) workshop to train potential leaders of Family Clusters. It includes four or five basic skillshops for learning skills and theory related to the Family Cluster model, as well as two demonstration sessions with families.

Labs and workshops are planned by Family Clustering, Inc., at a variety of locations in the United States, Australia, New Zealand, the Philippines, and elsewhere. They are often in affiliate sponsorship with agencies such as local church vestries, dioceses, and learning institutions. Catholic dioceses or groups of parishes can collaborate with Family Clustering to sponsor these events for their own local people or to direct their members to those already scheduled.

For further information on future training events, the reader should send a stamped, self-addressed, no. 10 envelope and request training event listings as they are updated; indicate which list you may already have. If you have no list at all, write to: Family Clustering, Inc., P.O. Box B, Chautauqua, NY 14722; telephone: (716) 357-3117.

In addition to her own training experiences, Dr. Margaret Sawin, the program's founder, is involved in producing an ongoing series of video programs, *Strengthening Families*, illustrating methods for enriching family experience for interpersonal growth. Information about this series is available from: FJC-Intellimedia, Inc., P.O. Box 6632, Syracuse, NY 13217-6632.

Interest in bible study among Catholics has grown tremendously in recent years. Small study, sharing, and prayer groups have formed officially or unofficially throughout the Archdiocese of Seattle as well as in other dioceses. Many Catholics have joined such groups not only in Catholic parishes but also in mainline Protestant and Evangelical churches.

Aware of this interest, parish adult education leaders have been seeking help in establishing scripture study groups and in choosing resource materials for these groups to use. Leaders are also recognizing the gap between those who receive Scripture in a tradition of interpretation and those who claim "Scripture alone" as the only measure of their faith.

With these needs in mind, a committee of persons with expertise in Scripture, both academic and practical, were asked to develop scripture guidelines for the Archdiocese of Seattle. The purpose of the guidelines is to assist those who are charged with the task of designing a scripture study program or forming small groups to study, share, and pray with Scripture. The guidelines attempt to answer two questions: (1) Is Catholic bible study different? and (2) How does one plan a Catholic scripture study program?

How is Roman Catholic Bible Study Different?

This section of the guidelines describes three elements of scripture study: (1) biblical spirituality; (2) revelation and inspiration; and (3) a Catholic approach to Scripture both in the way it is studied by scholars and its place within Roman Catholic tradition.

The normative spirituality for Catholics approaching Scripture is communal: God's revelation is to a people and it is within community that the people seek salvation. The Scriptures are the written expression of the community experience of God's people.

Catholics understand revelation as an ongoing process by which God continually shows what divinity means through the everyday lives of people. Scripture and tradition have been known as the two sources of revelation. However, current Catholic thought identifies tradition, or the continually evolving doctrines of the Church as taught by the bishops, as final authority within the Catholic community. The Bible is certainly a privileged source of Catholic life and faith, and the bishops have the duty of listening to it as such, but Scripture does not define the limits of Catholic teachings. As each generation of Catholic theologians seeks to understand the meaning of faith in a new period of history, Scripture serves as a major source, but not as the ultimate answer, for understanding contemporary issues and problems.

The Bible is the record of this revelation in a certain period of time, written for the sake of our salvation. Its inspiration is tied to the cultural, historical, and scientific characteristics of the times in which it was written.

Catholic biblical scholars use the same critical methods of biblical interpretation that other scholars use. Modern biblical scholars have devoted themselves to understanding the historical character of the biblical books. They make an effort to interpret the whole of a particular book

Guidelines for
the Study of
Scripture

Jane E. Beno

*Jane E. Beno is the former
coordinator of Adult
Education in the Archdiocese
of Seattle and a doctoral
student in Adult Education
at the University of
Vancouver.*

rather than isolated passages pulled out of context to support a particular doctrine or viewpoint. The difference is that the Bible is part of the Catholic faith, not the whole of it. Another interesting and important element of Catholic scripture study is that the Bible does not offer only one consistent theology or position on a given issue but is a rich collection of divergent theological and spiritual viewpoints, approaches, and ideas.

This section concludes with a chart that summarizes the main points of contrast between Roman Catholic teaching on Scripture and some popular beliefs. Each chapter within the section ends with a short list of related readings.

How To Plan Scripture Programs for Roman Catholics

The next section includes articles on understanding adult learning and assistance in designing an adult scripture program. The article on adult learning examines four assumptions underlying "andragogy" or the art and science of helping adults learn. The assumptions chosen are (1) self-concept; (2) life experience; (3) readiness to learn; and (4) orientation to learning.

Adults perceive themselves as independent, self-directed persons who have certain explicit learning needs. They also have many years of life experience that are often powerful resources for learning. The readiness of adults to learn is usually related to some situation in their lives or to their stage of development (e.g., new parents, mid-life crisis). And, adults usually enter learning situations to solve immediate problems or, at least, to develop answers for the near future. Implications of these assumptions for scripture study programs are drawn.

Designing an adult scripture program is related to planning any other adult program and includes the elements of assessing needs; setting goals and objectives; and choosing methodology, content, setting, and resources. A sample needs assessment tool is included. The article on choosing a method includes a comparison of five popular approaches to Christian education: (1) behavioral; (2) socialization; (3) faith development; (4) liberation; and (5) interpretation. It then suggests steps to follow in selecting an appropriate method. Related readings are listed throughout.

Resources

This section includes criteria for choosing resources, a survey of modern translations and versions of the Bible, and an extensive annotated bibliography. The survey of translations includes a historical chart tracing the Bible from the Hebrew manuscripts to today's various English versions. The bibliography is divided into the following sections:

- Introductions to the Bible;
- Single-volume commentaries;
- Commentaries/series;
- Biblical dictionaries;

- Concordances;
- Periodicals;
- Special topics;
- Individual books of the Bible;
- Reflection aids;
- Discussion aids;
- Audio-visual discussion aids;
- Study programs;
- Information on where to obtain other resources (including those in Spanish). This section includes the addresses of publishers whose books are listed in the guidelines.

How To Obtain

These *Guidelines for Scripture Study* are available from: F.C.D.D./Adult Education, Archdiocese of Seattle, 910 Marion Street, Seattle, WA 98104; cost: $5.00 each. The booklet is spiral-bound, 8½" by 11", contains 74 pages and was published in fall of 1985.

Developing Ministering Communities

Jacqueline McMakin and Rhoda Nary

"I've received so much. Now I want to give."

How often we hear these words from people whose faith has come alive through RCIA, RENEW, and other renewal efforts. These people are ready for ministry. They have experienced community and spiritual development through small faith-sharing groups and the process of the catechumenate and are now openly asking, "How can I build on my renewal experience?"

One answer, which we believe holds great promise for both the Church and the wider world, is: join or form a ministering community! Yes, this can provide a way to build on the spiritual nourishment and sense of community that people receive in RCIA and RENEW. It adds the vital third dimension of mission.

Ministering communities are not new. Jesus called people who shared his vision to join him in a community that had three dimensions. This involved learning to care for one another as friends (community), deepening their relationship with God (prayer), and extending Jesus' ministry of compassion and justice (mission).

Similarly, throughout history, certain people have articulated a particular vision and called others to that same vision. They joined together and offered their gifts in service of the ministries that evolved. Past examples are Francis of Assisi and George Fox, founder of the Quakers. Martin Luther King, Jr., Mother Theresa, and Elisabeth Kübler-Ross are more recent examples. There are many lesser known people who have done the same thing.

Through such programs as RCIA and RENEW much spiritual nourishment and community building have been happening. This has affected thousands of people and could result in an explosion of ministries.

However, in order for this to happen, people need assistance and support in moving from participation in faith-sharing groups to taking part in, or forming, ministering communities. To assist this movement, pastors, adult educators, and other parish leaders can offer parishioners four kinds of support.

1. Discernment

Sensitive, faithful people are aware of enormous numbers of needs around them or further from home. To which should they respond? How do they prevent what is being called "compassion fatigue"? How do they avoid the fragmentation that comes when they respond to too many needs and spread themselves too thinly?

The biblical mandate seems to be an invitation to be quiet, listen to God's call, and respond in faithfulness. In the familiar Mary and Martha story, Jesus reminds Martha not to worry about so many things but to attend to one thing well. In his description of a variety of ministries, Paul in Romans 12 suggests that if teaching is our ministry, "let us give all we have to our teaching," or "if it is serving others, let us concentrate on our service" (J.B. Phillips translation). In other words, we are being given permission to focus on the one ministry to which we are called

Jacqueline McMakin and Rhoda Nary are members of the Partners Community, an ecumenical group based in Washington, D.C., and consultants in spiritual development and lay ministry.

90

rather than being fretful about too many things, which results in feelings of powerlessness and guilt.

As a result of RCIA and RENEW, many people have learned about God's call to each person. However, important life questions remain: What is my specific calling to mission? What are the gifts God has given me to offer in this calling? What part of God's vision for the world is mine to carry and implement?

Our work has focused on helping people discern the ministries to which they feel called. We designed ways to begin addressing the important life questions mentioned above in a six-week course called "Discovering Your Ministry and Gifts." Not only does the course enable people to consider their gifts, calling, and vision, it helps them to find or develop structures in which to offer ministry and to see how these ministering communities tie in with the larger faith community of which they are a part.

Subsequently, course participants asked us to design other courses to give them a stronger background for ministry. Taking Jesus' life and work with his disciples as a model, we developed a first course to introduce people to the God whose call to people is recorded in the Old Testament. This was followed by a course called "Meeting Jesus in the New Testament," which challenges participants to make faith decisions based on Jesus' call to discipleship. The third course, "Tools for Christian Growth," offers training in some of the classic tools needed for growth as ministering Christians. These include reconciliation, healing, life style questions, and sharing our story. Together these courses are now being used as a ministry discernment and formation process in churches around the country and in Canada.[1]

Parish leaders can become familiar with a ministry discernment process such as ours and then offer it through different formats: in courses, retreats, workshops, or in counseling or informal conversations.

2. Structure

Once people have an idea of their particular calling, parish leaders can help them decide through what structure it can best be offered. Three possibilities that fit most people's situations are these:

a) Existing parish structures seen in a new light.   If a person feels called to ministry within the parish, there is often a committee, council, or task force already involved in that mission. When these groups are solely task oriented, they are prone to causing participant burnout. The study *How to Prevent Lay Leader Burnout*[2] showed that a key antidote to burnout is building time for spiritual nourishment and community building into every parish meeting (i.e., turning existing parish structures into ministering communities that integrate spiritual development, caring, and mission).

Take, for example, this conversation between John Heins, the president of one church's parish council, and a member of his church:

John: "I loved my year as president and received such great feedback."

1. Jacqueline McMakin and Rhoda Nary, *Doorways to Christian Growth* (Minneapolis, Minn.: Winston-Seabury Press, 1984).

2. Roy Oswald and Jacqueline McMakin, *How to Prevent Lay Leader Burnout* (Washington, D.C.: Alban Institute, 1984).

Member: "Why? I thought most people felt it was a drag to be on the council. What did you do differently?"

John: "I began each meeting with a substantial period of time for personal sharing and spiritual nourishment. We did a variety of things. Sometimes I passed around a beautiful stone or some other object and asked people to share, stream of consciousness, whatever occurred to them. At other times, someone would read a relevant Bible passage, and we talked in pairs about its implications for our work together. In our first meeting in September, we talked about a favorite vacation experience just to keep that relaxed vacation feeling going a bit longer."

Member: "But how did you get through the agenda? Didn't people worry about that and object to 'wasting time' in the way you described?"

John: "Not really. I guess I was enthusiastic and was obviously inviting people to do something that I found highly enjoyable and refreshing. That was part of it. And, then, if people get a chance to be heard at the beginning of the meeting and voice some of their deepest concerns, they have less need to make long-winded speeches during the meeting defending their point of view. There were real benefits to spending generous time in community building and spiritual development. The meetings went smoothly; we often sailed through the agenda; people were more mellow; and if we didn't complete an item or two, we simply postponed it or assigned a couple of people to take care of it in the interim. We had a great time together. And, I'm honestly sorry my time as president is over."

b) Ministry support groups. These are best for those people who feel called to an individual ministry outside the parish—in the home, on the job, or in the community—but who want their spiritual and personal support to come from fellow parishioners. For example, young mothers find that banding together in a community that supports their ministry in the home helps them with both the practical and spiritual dimensions of homemaking and children. Again, public school teachers in the same parish find the support they need from one another in order to be faithful and creative in the classroom. Parishes can provide help and support for people who have a common ministry, encouraging them to gather under the aegis of the parish to share concerns and to support each other.

c) Mission groups or servant communities. These are for people called to the same ministry, either within or beyond the parish. Two or more people can form such a group. Usually one person with a strong sense of vision articulates a particular way to implement that vision, which is shared by a few others who feel moved to join together. The variety of missions tackled by such groups is endless—addressing community hunger, running a retreat program for the parish, ministry to elderly shut-ins, tutoring inner-city students, preventing nuclear war.

Servant communities of this kind are amazing in their efficiency. Often composed of a handful of people, they can make an enormous difference. In our area, such groups have started low-income housing programs, social justice advocacy work, ecumenical renewal groups in churches. People who thrive in such groups are those who do not like a lot of structure and who want the autonomy and independence that this type of group affords.

Parish leaders can be aware of these three models for ministering communities. As they talk with people, they can be sensitive to the model that seems appropriate to that individual. They can publish articles in the parish newsletter to heighten parishioners' consciousness regarding these models. They can be on the lookout for people who are excited by this vision for ministry, enlisting their help in encouraging formation of ministering communities. In these ways, leaders can encourage the personal initiative of members who wish to form ministering communities and be ready to support them in their efforts.

3. Training and Resources

As people take part in ministering communities, they realize their need for specialized training and for other kinds of resources. Parish leaders can help by connecting these people with appropriate resources. It may be that people called to minister to the elderly need help in locating good study or reading material, or they might want some training in skills directly related to their mission. Perhaps, they may need seed money to start a project or to attend a conference. Those called to peace-making may need training in legislation analysis or nonviolent protest. People involved in evangelization may need to learn skills in listening and reconciliation, as they meet those who have been estranged from the churches. Pastors and adult educators can continually assess the community's needs for ministry and help provide appropriate resources for various forms of ministry.

4. Community Climate

One of the most important contributions parish staff and leaders can make to ministry development in the parish is to help provide an atmosphere of support and caring for this to happen. Like the artists in the Renaissance, all of us need others to act as our patrons, to recognize and value our gifts and vision, and to see that they are expressed in tangible forms. In our book, *Doorways to Christian Growth,* we devote an entire chapter to this important attitude and function, which can be carried out in many ways. Formally, recognition of good work well done at Sunday liturgies or in the parish newsletter is important. Allowing ministering people to offer reflections or short statements of witness during the liturgy is another way to affirm their callings. Informally, in conversations and gatherings, each parish member can show an interest in the gifts and ministries of others and thereby offer affirmation, encouragement, and support. Further, pastors can call the parish to ministry in their homilies and teaching and set a tone of possibility in the congregation.

Jesus called his disciples to come together to be with him in preparation for going out in ministry on their own. Their whole life together prepared them for ministry.

Similarly, the whole life of a parish community fosters ministry development, either directly or indirectly. Indeed, it is important to have a variety of ways to grow together, remembering that parishioners are in different places on a faith journey.

For cognitive, intellectual background and challenge, lecture/reading programs are important. In addition, a variety of small-group opportunities such as those offered by RCIA and RENEW give people a chance to be more personally involved in faith sharing. Ministry discernment and training programs assist people in identifying and developing ministries, which can then be offered through ministering communities. And, not to be forgotten is the need for plenty of "friendly open space," as Henri Nouwen puts it, for those who want to be or to rest at this point in their lives rather than to be engaged and involved.

Below is a diagram that illustrates the different places that people can be during their life of faith. Applying this to the parish, we can see at least six "rooms" that are needed to accommodate the many people within the parish home.

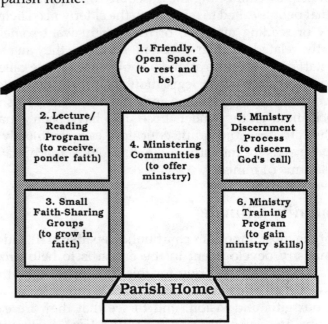

A diagram such as this is a helpful tool to analyze parish structures in order to ensure that there are a number of ways for people to grow in faith and develop ministries.

Such variety is nothing new. What has been missing, though, is the structure for ministry we are calling ministering communities. We believe they can harness the tremendous gifts and dedication of the laity, enabling the reign of God to be realized more fully in our time.

Jacqueline McMakin and Rhoda Nary are members of the Partners Community, a small ecumenical servant community committed to fostering faith development and ministry discernment among individuals and parishes. They are available for consultation, retreat and workshop leadership and may be reached at 1309 Merchant Lane, McLean, VA, 22101, (703) 827-0336.

A Regional RCIA

Eleanor Rae

During the past year, one of the issues that our diocesan committee for the implementation of the RCIA faced was the possibility of instituting the catechumenate on a regional basis. This issue was raised by some of the members who questioned as realistic the idea that each parish, no matter how limited its resources and interests, would actually establish a viable process for catechumens. Might it not be better, they reasoned, to establish regional catechumenates where they are needed, rather than have situations in which parishes are simply paying lip service to the RCIA? We decided that the next step in our process would be to undertake a survey of the dioceses in the United States to see if, in fact, regional catechumenates were already in existence and, if so, what were their positive and negative experiences in this area. Following are the results of this survey. But, before looking at the results, let me address the questionnaire itself, the recipients of the questionnaire, and the number of responses received by the committee.

The questionnaire, which we limited to one page, was concerned with issues such as the composition of the region; the reason for establishing the catechumenate on a regional basis; the locality for the celebration of the rites; the coordination between parishes; the involvement of leadership people, including the bishop, pastor, and parish staffs; and the issue of support for the neophyte. The respondents were also asked to identify the strengths and weaknesses of the regional catechumenate as they perceived it. A copy of the questionnaire (see Supplement 1) and a cover letter stating our purposes in requesting this information were sent to each diocese in the United States, addressed to the diocesan coordinator for the RCIA. Out of a total of 56 dioceses that responded (see Supplement 2), 12 indicated that they have (had) some form of a regionalized catechumenate. The dioceses responding positively were Manchester, Cleveland, Toledo, Youngstown, Indianapolis, Joliet, Des Moines, San Bernardino, San Francisco, Great Falls/Billings, Seattle, and Pueblo.

The questionnaire itself yielded the following information. The regionalization of the catechumenate (question 3) has occurred in both urban and rural areas. In the majority of cases, the catechumenate was instituted as the result of a regionally felt need or desire, rather than at the initiative of a diocese. Among the strong points listed as a result of the establishment of a regional RCIA process were the experience of Church as an enlarged faith community; a more effective use of both human and financial resources; the development of team ministry; the enablement of better group processes because of the numbers involved; the realization that, if the RCIA were not implemented on a regional basis, it probably would not be implemented at all; the cooperation that was realized among parishes; the enhanced organization (question 4).

The survey asked for identification of the weaknesses as well (question 5). The following were among those noted: organization is difficult; parish identity may be weak; the turnover of personnel; the lack of follow-up after initiation.

The next question (6) asked for the rationale behind the establishment of the regional cetechumenate. In the majority of cases, the catechumenate

Eleanor Rae, Ph.D., is the director of the Office of Laity in the Diocese of Bridgeport.

95

was regionalized for very practical reasons: to enable parishes that were not ready individually to begin the process as a team; as an additional step in an already established pattern of collaboration between parishes; as a practical response to the reality of limited resources. However, one region responded from a sense of ecclesiology—an understanding of Church as a larger community. The next question (7) was concerned with the location where the rites were celebrated. Two respondents said all rites were celebrated in the local parishes, while the remainder celebrated some rites locally and some in the cathedral. All of the responses indicated the use of a collaborative model of ministry among those responsible for the RCIA process, with this model at times facilitated by one team member (elected or appointed) and at other times the team as a whole shared responsibility for the process (questions 8, 9, 10). The final issue—that of the period of mystagogia (questions 11, 12)—was handled in one of two ways. In some instances, the individual parishes were totally responsible for this phase of the process. In other instances, a regional structure was formalized, which included support groups, celebrations, and encouragement for the neophytes in choosing a particular ministry in which to serve.

The intent of the survey was to help answer the question of the committee: Based on the experiences of dioceses that have undertaken the implementation of a regional catechumenate, is there reason to think that this is an approach worth pursuing? It is hoped that this sharing of our data will help other dioceses in their decision making as they face this issue.

(The author wishes to express her thanks to Mrs. Cathy Romano, a member of the committee for the implementation of the RCIA in the Diocese of Bridgeport, for gathering the data on which this article is based.)

Supplement 1

Rite of Christian Initiation of Adults Regional Catechumenate Survey

1. Name of diocese _____

2. Is there a Regional Catechumenate in your diocese?
   YES_____   NO_____

3. What is the composition of the region?

4. What are its strong points?

5. What are its weak points?

6. Why was it established?

7. Where are the rites celebrated?

   Local parishes _____
   Cathedral _____
   Other _____

8. How is it coordinated between parishes?

9. Is there a CORE Group?

10. What part does the bishop, pastor, staff members of the parishes play?

11. How do you continue to support after initiation?

12. How is community for the initiated developed and maintained?

13. Your Name: _____

    Address: _____

Supplement 2

Dioceses in the United States Responding to the Survey

REGION I (New England States)

Bridgeport
Burlington
Manchester*
Portland
Springfield

REGION II (New York State)

Brooklyn
New York
Ogdensburg
Rockville Centre
Syracuse

REGION III (Pennsylvania, New Jersey)

Erie
Harrisburg
Metuchen
Newark

REGION IV (Delaware, Florida, Georgia, Maryland, North & South Carolina, Virginia, West Virginia, Washington, D.C., Virgin Islands)

Raleigh
Richmond

REGION V (Alabama, Kentucky, Louisiana, Mississippi, Tennessee)

Alexandria/Shreveport
Louisville
Memphis
Mobile
Nashville
New Orleans

REGION VI (Michigan, Ohio)

Cincinnati
Cleveland*
Detroit
Kalamazoo
Marquette
Toledo*
Youngstown*

REGION VII (Illinois, Indiana, Wisconsin)

Green Bay
Indianapolis*

*Indicates positive response to question of regional catechumenate.

Joliet*
Lafayette
Madison
Superior

REGION VIII (Minnesota, North & South Dakota)

St. Paul/Minneapolis

REGION IX (Iowa, Kansas, Nebraska, Missouri)

Des Moines*
Grand Island
Jefferson City
Springfield/Cape Girardeau

REGION X (Arkansas, Oklahoma, Texas)

Beaumont
Fort Worth
Lewisville
Victoria

REGION XI (California, Hawaii, Nevada, Pacific Islands)

Reno/Las Vegas
San Bernardino*
San Diego
San Francisco*

REGION XII (Alaska, Idaho, Montana, Oregon, Washington)

Baker
Great Falls/Billings*
Seattle*
Spokane

REGION XIII (Arizona, Colorado, New Mexico, Utah, Wyoming)

Cheyenne
Las Cruces
Pueblo*
Salt Lake City

*Indicates positive response to question of regional catechumenate.

TOPICAL INDEX (1982—1987)

Scripture Study Program: Diocese of Little Rock / 1985–86:88
  James O'Leary
Suggestions on Facilitating Learning about the Soviet Union / 1985–86:81
  Cynthia Scott
The Living Edge of Christianity / 1984–85:93
  Michael C. O'Callaghan
The Role of Imagination and Phantasy in Adult Religious
Education / 1985–86:3
  Charles F. Piazza
Theological and Pastoral Reflections on the Studies of Matthew, Luke,
and John in the Church of Memphis, Tennessee / 1982:36
  Robert E. Obach

Adult Learning (Theory)
Ministry to Adults in a Changing World / 1987
  Gregory Michael Smith
Theory of Christian Adult Education Methodology / 1982:9
  Malcolm S. Knowles
Fostering Adult Faith: An Integrated Approach / 1987
  Charles F. Piazza

Adult Religious Education (Diocesan)

An Archdiocesan Council for Adult Education: How It Can Make a
Difference / 1982:43
  Diana Bader, OP

C.A.R.E.: A Diocesan-wide Approach to Grass-Roots Adult Religious
Education / 1982:52
  Joseph Crisafulli

Chicago Archdiocesan Center of CCD/Adult Division: One Model of
Multicultural Catechesis / 1982:49
  Chicago Archdiocesan Adult Education Staff

Adult Religious Education (Foundations for)

Adult Education in Church Documents / 1982:3
  Mariella Frye, MHSH

Foundations: The Scope, Purposes, and Goals of Adult Religious
Education / 1983:17
  Leon McKenzie

Integration of the Story: A Philosophical Foundation for Adult Religious
Education / 1984–85:20
  Matthew J. Hayes
Tensions between Adult Growth and Church Authority / 1982:21
  James R. Schaefer

Adult Religious Education (Parish)

Adult Religious Education: Moving from Rhetoric to Reality / 1985–86:55
  H. Richard McCord

Developing Ministering Communities / 1987
  Jacqueline McMakin and Rhoda Nary

Parish Adult Religious Education: A Survey of Practice / 1985–86:45
Matthew J. Hayes

Fostering Adult Faith: An Integrated Approach / 1987
Charles F. Piazza

Project: Beginning a Parish Committee of Adult Catechesis / 1982:64
Jacques Weber, SJ

The Adult Religious Educator in Service to Parish Renewal / 1983:37
H. Richard McCord, Jr.

The Rights of Adults in the Church / 1983:35
Gregory Michael Smith

Three Challenges for Adult Educators / 1984–85:40
James M. Sherer

Who is Responsible for Adult Religious Education? / 1987
James DeBoy

Adult Religious Education (Research in)

Parish Adult Religious Education: A Survey of Practice / 1985–86:45
Matthew J. Hayes

Australia

Adult Education Down Under: Some Reflections / 1984–85:55
Andrea Flake

Bibliographies

A Selected Annotated Bibliography on Adult Religious
Eduction / 1982:73
Mary Leonard Donovan, SHF, and Joseph P. Sinwell

A Select Annotated Bibliography on the RCIA for Adult Religious
Educators / 1984–85:102
Karen M. Hinman

A Selected Annotated Bibliography on Stages of Adult
Development / 1982:75
Loretta Girzaitis

A Selected Annotated Bibliography on Working with
Volunteers / 1982:77
James M. Sherer

Justice and Peace: A Bibliographic Survey for Adult Religious
Educators / 1984–85:116
Maurice L. Monette, OMI

Resources for a Basic Study of Television / 1983:62
John Miller

Resources for Implementing the Bishops' Pastoral Letter on
War and Peace / 1984–85:119
Catherine I. Adlesic

Calling Ministry

The Calling and Caring Ministry / 1985–86:113
Christine Liegey, PBVM

Campus Ministry

Campus Ministry and Adult Education: A Reflection / 1985–86:21
Peter K. Meehan

Canon Law

The Revised Code of Canon Law: An Adult Perspective / 1985–86:10
Kenneth E. Lasch

Church (Authority)

Tensions between Adult Growth and Church Authority / 1982:21
James R. Schaefer

Church (Documents)

Adult Education in Church Documents / 1982:3
Mariella Frye, MHSH

Clergy Education

The Use of Adult Learning Theory in the Continuing Education of the
Clergy / 1983:44
Rev. Edward J. Mahoney

Contemporary Trends

Change and Society: Challenges for the Adult Educator / 1984–85:67
Loretta Girzaitis

Conversion Processes

Facilitating Conversion Processes / 1987
Robert J. Hater

Facilitator Training

Effective Leadership Training for Renewal Groups / 1984–85:85
Daniel S. Mulhall

Family

A Family Sensitivity in Adult Religious Education / 1987
Thomas F. Lynch

Family Clusters: An Environment for Adult Growth / 1987
Joseph Crisafulli

Formation of Ministers

Basic Formation of Parish Ministers of Adult Education: A
Module / 1983:21
Jacques Weber, SJ

Ministerial Development Program: Diocese of Boise / 1985–86:99
Ellen Bush, CSC, and Michael Reifel

Planning Creative Adult Religious Education Leadership
Programs / 1987
Charles F. Piazza and M. Sheila Collins

The Challenge of Lay Ministry Formation / 1983:33
Dolores R. Leckey

Pastoral Ministry Formation: A Diocesan Response / 1987
Peter R. Bradley and Edna Friedenbach

Fundamentalism

The Problem of Catholic Fundamentalism / 1984–85:81
Jacques Weber, SJ

Imagination

Models and Hints in Using Phantasies in Adult Religious
Education / 1985–86:77
Charles F. Piazza

The Role of Imagination and Phantasy in Adult Religious
Education / 1985–86:3
Charles F. Piazza

Inactive Catholics

Outreach to the Inactive Catholic / 1985–86:109
Rebecca Miller

Independent Learning

Independent Learning: The Untapped Resource / 1985–86:25
Richard M. Lawless

Justice and Peace

Educating for Justice and Peace: Home, Parish and Community /
1985–86:17
Michael True

Justice and Peace: Bibliographic Survey for Adult Religious
Educators / 1984–85:116
Maurice L. Monette, OMI

Learning in Faith about the Soviet Union / 1985–86:59
Cynthia Scott

Resources for Implementing the Bishops' Pastoral Letter on
War and Peace / 1984–85:119
Catherine I. Adlesic

Three Challenges for Adult Educators / 1984–85:40
James M. Sherer

Marriage

Called to Love: A Program for the Newly Married / 1984–85:89
Francis J. Schweigert

Marriage: A Continuing Wedding Celebration / 1982:87
Clarisse Croteau-Chonka

Mentors

The Adult as Mentor / 1984–85:25
Gregory Michael Smith

Multicultural Ministry

Chicago Archdiocesan Center of CCD/Adult Division: One Model of
Multicultural Catechesis / 1982:49
Chicago Archdiocesan Adult Education Staff

Ministering to the Adult as Learner in the Black Community /
1984–85:47
Dorothy Giloley, SSJ

Multicultural Adult Catechesis: What Is It and for Whom? / 1983:23
Marina Herrera

The Spirituality of the Black Catholic Adult / 1987
Greer G. Gordon

Principles of Adult Learning, the RCIA, and the Black Catholic / 1987
Greer G. Gordon

Needs Assessment

A Different Approach to Needs Assessment / 1987
Matthew J. Hayes

Doing a Needs Assessment / 1982:109
James M. Sherer

Needs Assessment: The Basis of Program Planning / 1982:33
Leon McKenzie

Parenting Education

A New Philosophy and Theology of Parent Education for the
1980s / 1983:10
Mary Jane Saia and Judith M. Boyle

Educating for Justice and Peace: Home, Parish, and Community /
1985–86:17
Michael True

New Directions for Parent Education Programs / 1983:28
Mary Jane Saia and Judith M. Boyle

The Role of Parents in Sacramental Preparation / 1985–86:35
Kathleen Bierne, PBVM

Working Effectively with Parents in Sacramental Preparation / 1985–86:39
Kathy Finley

Parish Renewal

Effective Leadership Training for Renewal Groups / 1984–85:85
Daniel S. Mulhall

From Head to Heart and Beyond: A Faith Journey / 1984–85:61
Gerard P. and Mary Ellen Mandry

Our Journey in Faith: Renewal in the Making / 1985–86:93
Alice Stefaniak

Program Development: A Community Process / 1985–86:30
Margaret N. Ralph

Rebuilding Our Pluralistic Parishes: The Adult Educator's
Challenge / 1984–85:74
John R. Zaums

The Adult Religious Educator in Service to Parish Renewal / 1983:37
H. Richard McCord, Jr.

Principles of Adult Learning, the RCIA, and the Black Catholic / 1987
  Greer G. Gordon

Rights of Adults

The Rights of Adults in the Church / 1983:35
  Gregory Michael Smith

Sacramental Preparation

The Role of Parents in Sacramental Preparation / 1985–86:35
  Kathleen Bierne, PBVM

Working Effectively with Parents in Sacramental Preparation / 1985–86:39
  Kathy Finley

Scripture Study

Adults and the Study of Scripture in the Church / 1985–86:83
  Frank C. Bates

Guidelines for the Study of Scripture / 1987
  Jane E. Beno

Parish Bible Study: Generator of Renewal / 1983:54
  Eugene F. Trester

Scripture Study Program: Diocese of Little Rock / 1985–86:88
  James O'Leary

Theological and Pastoral Reflections on the Studies of Matthew, Luke,
and John in the Church of Memphis, Tennessee / 1982:36
  Robert E. Obach

Single Adults

Ministry with Single Adults / 1983:25
  Brigid M. O'Donnell

Social Justice

Building the Kingdom of God / 1987
  Mary Lou Durall

Soviet Union

Learning in Faith about the Soviet Union / 1985–86:59
  Cynthia Scott

Suggestions on Facilitating Learning about the Soviet Union / 1985–86:81
  Cynthia Scott

Spirituality

All about Prayer / 1982:96
  Clarisse Croteau-Chonka

Prayer: A Special Challenge for Adult Religious Education / 1983:31
  Clarisse Croteau-Chonka

Prayer: Styles of Being with God / 1983:60
  Clarisse Croteau-Chonka

The Eye of the Needle/The Light at the End of the Tunnel: A
Contemplative Spirituality for Religious Educators / 1985–86:66
  Virginia Sullivan Finn

Feeding the Hunger: The Center for Spiritual Development / 1987
  Ann Marie Wallace

Video

Resources for a Basic Study of Television / 1983:62
  John Miller

Video Programming in Adult Religious Education: A New
Frontier / 1984–85:96
  Joseph P. Sinwell

Volunteers

A Selected Annotated Bibliography on Working with
Volunteers / 1982:77
  James M. Sherer

The Ministry of Volunteers in Adult Religious Education / 1982:66
  H. Richard McCord

AUTHOR INDEX (1982—1987)

Adlesic, Catherine I.

Implementation of the Pastoral Letter on War and Peace / 1984–85:52

Resources for Implementing the Bishops' Pastoral Letter on War and Peace / 1984–85:119

Bader, Diana, OP

An Archdiocesan Council for Adult Education: How It Can Make a Difference / 1982:43

Genesis 2: Is It Harmful to Your Spiritual Health? / 1982:120

A Review of *More Radiant Than Noonday* by Loretta Girzaitis / 1982:124

Bates, Frank C.

Adults and the Study of Scripture in the Church / 1985–86:83

Beno, Jane E.

Guidelines for the Study of Scripture / 1987

Bierne, Kathleen, PBVM

The Role of Parents in Sacramental Preparation / 1985–86:35

Boyle, Judith M. and Mary Jane Saia

A New Philosophy and Theology of Parent Education for the 1980s / 1983:10

New Directions for Parent Education Programs / 1983:28

Bradley, Peter R., and Edna Friedenbach

Pastoral Ministry Formation: A Diocesan Response / 1987

Bush, Ellen, CSC

Adult Catechesis in the Diocese of Boise / 1985–86:31

Bush, Ellen, CSC, and Michael Reifel

Ministerial Development Program: Diocese of Boise / 1985–86:99

Chicago Archdiocesan Adult Education Staff

Chicago Archdiocesan Center of CCD/Adult Division: One Model of Multicultural Catechesis / 1982:49

Crisafulli, Joseph

C.A.R.E.: A Diocesan-wide Approach to Grass-Roots Adult Religious Education / 1982:52

Family Clusters: An Environment for Adult Growth / 1987

Croteau-Chonka, Clarisse

All about Prayer / 1982:96

Marriage: A Continuing Wedding Celebration / 1982:87

Prayer: A Special Challenge for Adult Religious Education / 1983:31

Prayer: Styles of Being with God / 1983:60

DeBoy, James

Who Is Responsible for Adult Religious Education? / 1987

Donovan, Mary Leonard, SHF, and Joseph P. Sinwell

A Selected Annotated Bibliography on Adult Religious Education / 1982:73

Dunning, James B.

Method Is the Medium Is the Message: Catechetical Method in the Rite of Christian Initiation of Adults / 1983:14

Dunwoody, Gregory

The First Five Minutes / 1982:42

Durall, Mary Lou

Building the Kingdom of God / 1987

Elias, John L.

Adult Religious Education and the Emerging Field of Adult Studies / 1982:6

Ecclesial Models of Adult Religious Education / 1983:3

The Adult Journey in Faith / 1984–85:12

Finley, Kathy

Working Effectively with Parents in Sacramental Preparation / 1985–86:39

Finn, Virginia Sullivan

The Eye of the Needle/The Light at the End of the Tunnel: A Contemplative Spirituality for Religious Educators / 1985–86:66

Flake, Andrea

Adult Education Down Under: Some Reflections / 1984–85:55

Flattery, John J.

The Promise of Our Possibilities / 1982:54

Frye, Mariella, MHSH

Adult Education in Church Documents / 1982:3

Giloley, Dorothy, SSJ

Ministering to the Adult as Learner in the Black Community / 1984–85:47

Girzaitis, Loretta

A Selected Annotated Bibliography on Stages of Adult Development / 1982:75

Professional Associations for the Adult Educator / 1983:66

Change and Society: Challenges for the Adult Educator / 1984–85:67

Gordon, Greer G.

Principles of Adult Learning, the RCIA, and the Black Catholic / 1987

The Spirituality of the Black Catholic Adult / 1987

Hater, Robert J.

Facilitating Conversion Processes / 1987

Hayes, Matthew J.

A Different Approach to Needs Assessment / 1987

Integration of the Story: A Philosophical Foundation for Adult Religious Education / 1984–85:20

Parish Adult Religious Education: A Survey of Practice / 1985–86:45

Herrera, Marina

Multicultural Adult Catechesis: What Is It and for Whom? / 1983:23

Hinman, Karen M.

A Select Annotated Bibliography on the RCIA for Adult Religious Educators / 1984–85:102

Hughes, Jane Wolford

Adult Educators and Their Life-giving Challenge / 1985–86:70

Kleis, Russell J.

Survival of the Adult Educator / 1982:58

Knowles, Malcolm S.

A Theory of Christian Adult Education Methodology / 1982:9

Lasch, Kenneth E.

The Revised Code of Canon Law: An Adult Perspective / 1985–86:10

Lawless, Richard M.

Independent Learning: The Untapped Resource / 1985–86:25

Leckey, Dolores R.

The Challenge of Lay Ministry Formation / 1983:33

Leffel, Linda G.

The Design and Preparation of Effective Brochures / 1983:56

Liegey, Christine, PBVM

The Calling and Caring Ministry / 1985–86:113

Lynch, Thomas F.

A Family Sensitivity in Adult Religious Education / 1987

Lyons, James P.

Extended Learnings: The Religious Right / 1985–86:105

Mahoney, Edward J.

The Use of Adult Learning Theory in the Continuing Education of the Clergy / 1983:44

Mandry, Gerard P. and Mary Ellen

From Head to Heart and Beyond: A Faith Journey / 1984–85:61

McCord, H. Richard

The Ministry of Volunteers in Adult Religious Education / 1982:66

The Adult Religious Educator in Service to Parish Renewal / 1983:37

Adult Religious Education: Moving from Rhetoric to Reality / 1985–86:55

McKenzie, Leon

Needs Assessment: The Basis of Program Planning / 1982:33

Foundations: The Scope, Purposes, and Goals of Adult Religious Education / 1983:17

McMakin, Jacqueline and Rhoda Nary

Developing Ministering Communities / 1987

Meehan, Peter K.

Campus Ministry and Adult Education: A Reflection / 1985–86:21

Miller, John

Resources for a Basic Study of Television / 1983:62

Miller, Rebecca

Outreach to the Inactive Catholic / 1985–86:109

Monette, Maurice L., OMI

Educational Planning: Responding Responsibly / 1982:17

Justice and Peace: A Bibliographic Survey for Adult Religious Educators / 1984–85:116

Mulhall, Daniel S.

Effective Leadership Training for Renewal Groups / 1984–85:85

Obach, Robert E.

Theological and Pastoral Reflections on the Studies of Matthew, Luke, and John in the Church of Memphis, Tennessee / 1982:36

O'Callaghan, Michael C.

The Living Edge of Christianity / 1984–85:93

O'Donnell, Brigid M.

Ministry with Single Adults / 1983:25

O'Leary, James

Scripture Study Program: Diocese of Little Rock / 1985–86:88

Parent, Neil A.

A Book of Note: *Learning How to Learn* by Robert M. Smith / 1984–85:124

Piazza, Charles F.

Fostering Adult Faith: An Integrated Approach / 1987

The Role of Imagination and Phantasy in Adult Religious Education / 1985–86:3

Models and Hints in Using Phantasies in Adult Religious Education / 1985–86:77

Piazza, Charles F. and M. Sheila Collins

Planning Creative Adult Religious Education Leadership Programs / 1987

Rae, Eleanor

A Regional RCIA / 1987

Ralph, Margaret N.

Program Development: A Community Process / 1985–86:30

Renewal Programs as Adult Religious Education / 1987

Reifel, Michael and Ellen Bush, CSC

Ministerial Development Program: Diocese of Boise / 1985–86:99

Saia, Mary Jane and Judith M. Boyle

A New Philosophy and Theology of Parent Education for the 1980s / 1983:10

New Directions for Parent Education Programs / 1983:28

Scapanski, Gene A.

Graduate Programs in Adult Education Ministry / 1983:46

Schaefer, James R.

Tensions between Adult Growth and Church Authority / 1982:21

Schweigert, Francis J.

Called to Love: A Program for the Newly Married / 1984–85:89

Scott, Cynthia

Learning in Faith about the Soviet Union / 1985-86:59

Suggestions on Facilitating Learning about the Soviet Union / 1985–86:81

Shaughnessy, Maureen, SC

A Review of *Christian Initiation Resources:* Rev. James B. Dunning, Deacon William J. Reedy, editors / 1982:126

Sherer, James M.

A Selected Annotated Bibliography on Working with Volunteers / 1982:77

Guide to Successful Planning / 1982:99

Doing a Needs Assessment / 1982:109

Genesis 2 in Five Session Formats / 1982:122

Three Challenges for Adult Educators / 1984–85:40

Sinwell, Joseph P.

Video Programming in Adult Religious Education: A New Frontier / 1984–85:96

Sinwell, Joseph P. and Mary Leonard Donovan, SHF

A Selected Annotated Bibliography on Adult Religious Education / 1982:73

Smith, Gregory Michael

The Rights of Adults in the Church / 1983:35

The Adult as Mentor / 1984–85:25

Ministry to Adults in a Changing World / 1987

Stefaniak, Alice

Our Journey in Faith: Renewal in the Making / 1985–86:93

Stewart, Joyce

Administration: An Enabling Ministry / 1983:41